PAPUA NEW GUINEA

Language in context

Grade 4

Teacher Resource Book

Tandi Jackson

Illustrated by Jeanette Baude

OXFORD

Contents

Introduction

This book has been set out to make easy reference links to the Student Book. The headings are the same as those in the Student Book and each task is in a separate box.

In Grade 4, teachers should be teaching 50% of the time in English and 50% of the time in Vernacular. There are icons to show instantly whether the task is in English or Vernacular, and to show the teacher which subject the task involves.

 Activity conducted in English.

 Activity conducted in Vernacular.

 Teacher-directed activity.

 Students read.

 Students mime or act.

 Students construct.

 Students draw or paint.

 Students sing or make up a song.

 Students write.

Teachers should use this book in conjunction with the Student Book. It explains more fully how to use the Student Book. It also gives other activities that can be used by the teacher for each topic.

At the beginning of each chapter there is a detailed unit summary chart listing each topic heading, the activities in the Student Book and the Teacher Book, and the objectives that are met. The following icons are used to indicate the language learning outcomes:

 Speaking  Listening  Reading  Writing

Teachers are expected to elaborate on some topics that are only briefly touched on in this book, and to include them in their own language programs.

Student Books have simple directions in English with a line underneath like this:

 ____

Teachers should translate the English direction into the local vernacular (tok ples) so the students can write this neatly into their books. The following year, when these books are used again, the translation will already be in place. Please ensure that students write the translation neatly so that it can be read easily by others in the following years.

Bridging Readers 1–16

These are to be used with the Student Book. These Readers are designed to fit into the topics and some reading activities for them are included in this book. There are four Readers for each chapter of the Student Book.

Learning outcomes: Language

The following Language Outcomes apply to the whole year's work.

Strand: Speaking and listening

Sub-strands

Production

4.1.1V Use a range of spoken text types for different audiences and purposes to present familiar and unfamiliar ideas.

4.1.1E Use a range of spoken text types for both familiar and unfamiliar topics.

Skills and strategies

4.1.2V Use oral skills and strategies to share ideas and information.

4.1.2E Use oral skills and strategies to respond to simple classroom and social situations.

Context and text

4.1.3V Identify how audience, purpose and topic account for differences in how language is used.

4.1.3E Compare how simple spoken English texts are different according to their audience and purpose.

Strand: Reading

Sub-strands

Production

4.2.1E Read simple text types and interact with the ideas and information from the texts.

Context and text

4.2.3E Identify how ideas and information are presented in simple written and picture texts.

Critical literacy

4.2.4E Identify ways in which language has been used in a range of text types to create a response from readers.

Strand: Writing

Sub-strands

Production

4.3.1V Plan and produce a range of text types to develop familiar and unfamiliar ideas and information.

4.3.1.E Plan and produce a range of text types in all genre categories to present ideas and information.

Skills and strategies

4.3.2V/E Apply writing skills and strategies to plan, write and edit own texts and those of peers.

Critical literacy

4.3.3E Demonstrate knowledge of a range of text types and their structures and language features.

4.3.4E Identify how people and things are represented in illustrations and written texts.

Me and my Wantoks

Learning outcomes

Topic: Community living

Strand: Community

4.1.1 Investigate the work people in communities undertake.
4.1.2 Explain behaviour that promotes good relationships in the wider community.
4.1.3 Evaluate community services and the roles and responsibilities related to them.
4.2.1 Describe ways goods and services are exchanged in the community.
4.3.1 Describe customs related to events of significance.

Topic: Mathematics

Money.
Money problems.
Traditional counting.

Topic: Sport

Plan a fun sports day.
Diary.

Topic: Art and craft

Packaging.

Topic: Music/drama

Write advertising jingles.
Play: Reader 3: Shopping for Shoes.

Unit summary

Topics	Pictures and oral discussions	Student Book activities	Teacher Book activities	Cross-curriculum objectives	Language objectives
My wantoks' jobs	Discuss jobs.	Choose correct word. Answer questions.		Community living 4.1.1	Choose correct word. Describe wantoks.
Whose job?	Discuss pictures.	Match tools with jobs.	Phrases.	Community living 4.1.1	Matching. 4.1.1 E
Working for the government	Discuss government jobs.	Survey. Table. Match tools with jobs.	Job lists. Alphabetical order.	Community living 4.1.1 Graph	Alphabetical order.
Reader 1: What Will I Be When I Grow Up?	Read story together.		New vocabulary. Answer questions about story. Discuss rules of the road.	Community living 4.1.1	4.1.1 E 4.2.1 E
A small business	Discuss coconut products and processes.	Make coconut oil.	Making products. Marketing.	Community living 4.1.1	Following directions 4.1.3 E Recount/ procedural text.
Reader 2: Rina's Job	Read story together.		New vocabulary. Answer questions about story. Opposites.	Community living 4.1.1	Opposites. 4.1.2 E 4.2.1 E
Starting a small business	Discuss what you could sell.	Logos. Packaging.	Practical. Discuss wantok system.	Crafts. 4.1.1	4.1.1 E Advertising
Things we do together	Discuss what students do with wantoks.	Write.	Role-playing. Discuss special occasions.	Community living 4.1.2	4.3.1 V
Playing sport together	Discuss pictures.	Write a report.	Plan a fun sports day. Diary.	Sport. 4.1.2	Report. 4.3.1 V

Topics	Pictures and oral discussions	Student Book activities	Teacher Book activities	Cross-curriculum objectives	Language objectives
Money	Discuss old and new money.	Draw money.	Coin rubbings. Money problems.	Mathematics: money. 4.2.1	4.1.1 E
Banks	Discuss bank deposits and withdrawals.	Draw and fill in forms.		Mathematics: money.	Filling in forms. 4.1.2 E
A happy memory	Discuss story map.	Study story map. Plan and write story.	When who where why what. Read stories to class.		Recount. 4.3.3 V
Things we need	Discuss pictures.	Classify items.	Make lists. Draw items on list.	Community living 4.2.1	Classification. 4.3.1 E
Shopping	Discuss pictures.	Practise sentences.	Role-playing shopping phrases.	Community living 4.2.1	E Phrases.
Reader 3: Shopping for Shoes: A Play	Read text together.		Act the play. New vocabulary. Opposites. Problems.	Money. Drama.	4.1.2 E 4.2.1 E
Advertising	Discuss advertisement.	Make up an advertisement.	Advertisements. Jingles.	Music.	Advertisements. Adjectives.
Sharing	Discuss picture.	Discuss sharing with wantoks.		Community living 4.2.1	4.1.1 E
Trading	Discuss trade/ barter.	Bartering.	Barter party.	Community living 4.2.1	
Traditional trading: The Kula trade	Read and discuss.	Words that don't belong.	Bagi necklaces. Questions. Silent letters.	Culture 4.2.1	Questions. Silent letters. 4.1.2 V
Moka pig exchange	Read and discuss.	Write about ceremony.	Highland neck adornments.	Culture 4.2.1	4.1.2 V

Me and my Wantoks

Topics	Pictures and oral discussions	Student Book activities	Teacher Book activities	Cross-curriculum objectives	Language objectives
Reader 4: Fun at the Pigsty	Read story together.		New vocabulary. Answer questions about story.	4.1.2	Comprehension 4.2.1 E
At the market	Discuss picture.	Add ing to verbs. Classify.	Make a shopping list. Write about improving local marketplace.	Community living 4.2.1	
Looking after other places in the community	Discuss.		Make a table. Questions.	Community living 4.1.3	Making a table 4.1.2 V
Traditional counting	Study pictures.	Draw body. Numbers.	Counting to 50 by 1's, 2's and 5's.	Mathematics.	
Cargo cults	Discuss picture.	Choose the right word.	Giving opinions.	Culture 4.3.1	Opinions 4.1.4 E

Me and my wantoks

Explain: **self-employed** means working for yourself.
Salary is the money a person gets paid (the same amount each week) to work for someone else.

My wantoks' jobs

Answers:

Aunty Meri works in the **town**.
She is an office worker for Telikom.
Uncle Peta is a **builder**.
He builds houses for a big company.

This is Amo. He is an old **man**.
He is a village elder.
He looks after the **village**.
He likes **fishing**.

Jon runs a **trade store**.
His wife Ana works in the store.
They sell food and clothes to the people in the **village**.
They work very hard.

Sela and Bili have a **small** business.
They keep **pigs** in a piggery.
They feed the pigs food scraps, coconut meat and corn from the **garden**.
They **sell** the pigs to a butcher in town.

Rina works at a clothing shop. She is called a **shop** assistant.
She sells clothes to people.
She has to be **nice** to customers.
She **likes** Jimi.

Jimi is a **driver** for a big company.
He drives a bulldozer.
He makes **roads**.
He **likes** Rina.

Elizabeth and Kena **own** a PMV.
Elizabeth **banks** the money and cleans the PMV.
Kena **drives** the PMV.
Many village people **use** this service.

Uncle Sam and Aunty Grace grow **coconuts**.
They make coconut **kerosene**.
They also make **cooking** oil.
Aunty Grace makes **soap** out of coconuts.

This is Pastor John. He is the minister of our **church**.
He takes church services every **Sunday**.
He marries people and takes **funerals**.
He **teaches** people about God and his son Jesus.
He lives in our **village** with his wife, Jeni.

Whose job?

Whose job do these things belong to?

1 mask, white coat, stethoscope: **doctor**

2 tractor, spade, axe: **farmer**

3 needle, scissors, material, pins: **sewer**

4 apron, stove, food, white hat: **chef/cook**

5 blue uniform, hat, black shoes, badge: **policeman**

6 uniform, helmet, hose, ladder: **fireman**

Teaching English

Here are some **phrases** to do with getting work:

It's not easy **to find work.**

I'd like to do **that kind of work.**

It's not easy **to make a living.**

I've been **offered a job.**

I would like to **take on that job.**

Working for the government

Answers:
My mum works for the government. She is a **nurse**.
Mrs Bulabula works for the government. She is a **teacher**.
Kira works for the government. He is a **policeman**.

Answers:
Sink and taps: **plumber**
Paint and paintbrush: **painter**
Pills and syringe: **doctor**
Flowers and paper: **florist**
Phone and pen: **receptionist**
Computer and desk: **manager**
Blackboard and chalk: **teacher**

 **E** Show and discuss a list of government jobs.

Civil engineer – builds and maintains roads and bridges.

Librarian – works in the library with books.

Accountant – looks after accounts or money records.

Scientist – studies science and makes discoveries.

Laboratory technician – works with scientists in a laboratory.

Computer programmer – makes programs for computers.

Policeman – is in charge of law and order.

Nurse – looks after sick people.

Occupational therapist – helps people strengthen their limbs.

Health educator – teaches people about keeping healthy.

Dentist – looks after peoples' teeth.

Firefighter – puts out fires.

Horticulturalist – knows about growing plants.

Labourer – does physical work like digging drains.

Project manager – is the person in charge of a job.

Office assistant – works for the manager.

Driver – drives vehicles.

Painter – paints buildings.

Electrician – fixes electrical things.

Accounts clerk – looks after the money books in an office.

Architect – designs buildings.

Building inspector – inspects buildings to make sure they are well-built.

Bus driver – drives buses.

Forester – looks after the forest.

Town planner – plans the town.

Airport communications officer – uses computers at the airport.

  Discuss with students which of these jobs they would like to do and why.

  Discuss jobs held by students' family members and wantoks. What do their jobs entail?

E Ask students to put some of the above jobs into alphabetical order.

READER 1: What Will I Be When I Grow Up?

Read the story with the students.

New vocabulary: **stethoscope**, **medicine**, **hospital**, **study**, **mechanic**, **engines**, **librarian**, **computer**, **carefully**, **driver's licence**, **elementary**, **builder**, **rotten**, **pastor.**

Discuss the meanings of difficult words. Students should work out what they mean from context clues or illustrations.

Find a word in the text that means 'repair'. (fix)

Discuss the rules of the road. There must be rules on the road or people would crash. We must learn these rules before we can get a driver's licence.

A small business

E Read the methods with the students and discuss. If possible, get some coconuts and make coconut kerosene, cooking oil and soap.

Coconut products

Study pictures of these products with the students and then have them close their books. Ask students to describe how these were made:

Coconut kerosene

Coconut cooking oil

Coconut soap

How you can make coconut oil

 **E** Make some coconut oil with the students.

E Students could write a **recount** afterwards, explaining what they did, or they could write a **procedural text** explaining how to make coconut oil.

Marketing
Students are to discuss marketing the coconut oil they have made. They should answer these questions and complete the activities.

Could you sell this product?

Clean a small bottle with a lid or cork to keep your oil in. (Recycling)

Design a label to stick onto the bottle.

Give your product a name.

Write down the ingredients.

Write down what it can be used for.

Say where it is made.

Would this product sell at the market? Would it sell in the shops?

Could you get enough bottles?

How much could you sell it for? When deciding the price, think of the cost of the ingredients and the time it took you to make it.

Can you find some other friends who would like to start a small business with you, and make this product after school?

 READER 2: Rina's Job

Read the story with the students and discuss.

New vocabulary: **assistant**, **customers**, **choose**, **colour**, **asked**, **bright**, **could**, **undress**, **trouble**, **probably**, **stuck**, **easy**.

What was Rina trying to tell the fat lady?

Find the sentences that she didn't finish and write down what she may have said. For example: "Yes, but … (this dress is too small for you.")

Why did Jimi think that Rina had an easy job?

Is Rina's job easy? Why/why not?

Teaching English

Add **un** to these words to make them opposites:

dress do stuck tidy load lucky like told truth well

Starting a small business

Discuss with students what things they could make to sell. Divide them into small groups to do this. When each group has thought of something, tell them to do **For you to do**.

How do village businesses survive the wantok system? Discuss this story with the students. What do they think should be done?

> One village man and his wife were specialist producers of good quality tobacco. It was cured and stored in betel nut leaf-sheath bundles. Everyone recognised their 'brus' as being the best and plentiful throughout the whole year. It was understood that the couple would sell the bundles outside the village.

However, wantoks expected to be able to get a handout from the couple if their tobacco crop was not as good and there was a shortage of tobacco later in the year.

This couple worked harder than anyone else in the village to get a good crop. If they have to give their product to their wantoks for nothing, there is no reason to work hard and be successful. They will never get ahead.

Things we do together

  Have a discussion about what the students do at home with their wantoks.

  Students could do some role-playing.

  Ask them to write down the things they do and draw pictures.

  **Discuss** things we do as a community at church:

Special occasions like weddings, funerals and baptisms.

Other things like an Easter play or a Christmas play

A church fair, where people sell things to raise money for the church.

Playing sport together

 Choose students to read out what the people are saying in the speech bubbles.

 Use all this information to write a **report**.

For example:

Last week a football match, organised by .... (make up a name), was played at .... village. The adults played the children and they all had lots of fun.

Jon nearly got a try but he tripped over Simon and lost the ball.

Jimi kicked three goals for the adults but missed one. The adults were winning at half-time.

A funny thing happened when Kali tackled his Uncle Peta and pulled his shorts down. Everyone laughed and shouted.

After the second half, Kali scored a try and then Simon kicked the winning goal just before the whistle blew for the end of the game.

It was a great game and everyone enjoyed themselves.

Plan a **Fun Sports Day** at your village or community.
Refer to the Grade 3 Student Book, Chapter 2, page 58, **'Sports Day at the River'**.

Students could plan some novelty events for the adults. For example:

An egg and spoon race – a person has to place an egg or a lemon in a spoon and run with it. If it falls, they must pick it up and put it back into the spoon before they continue the race.

A three-legged race – two people each put an arm around the other's waist and tie their middle legs together. They must run together like this.

A sack race – a person has to climb into a sugar sack and try to race by jumping with their legs inside the sack. If you can get big sacks, two people can fit inside.

Balls in a bucket – a person must stand behind a line five metres away from a bucket and try to throw four balls into the bucket.

Students are to write letters to their wantoks inviting them to the Fun Sports Day, saying when and where it is to be held.

Spending time with my family and friends

E Students should make up a diary for the coming week. For homework, ask the students to write in the times spent with their family and friends, telling what they did. It might look something like this:

My diary

Monday	Tuesday	Wednesday	Thursday	Friday	Saturday	Sunday
Bathed Jenifa before school.	Emptied the rubbish bin.	Collected bottles from the rubbish to sell.	Swept around the house before school.	Took Aunty Meri some eggs.	Went to town to buy some shoes with Mum.	Went to church with the family.
Played with Jenifa after school.	Took my pet turtle some rice.	Went swimming after school with Maria and Pia.	Cleaned the truck for Dad.	Collected firewood with Maria.	Went to the market with Mum and Dad.	Played with my cousins on the beach.
Fed the hens with scraps.	Helped Mum to bake some bread.	Played soccer with Simon and Kali.	Took some bananas to Laena.	Helped Mum in the vegetable garden.	Watched a video at Lani's house.	Caught fish for my pet turtle.

Ask them what they did last week to help someone else in their community. They could make a list like this:

Monday: Bathed the baby and fed the hens.

Tuesday: Emptied the rubbish bin and helped Mum make bread.

Thursday: Swept around the house and cleaned the truck for Dad.

Friday: Took Aunty Meri some eggs and collected firewood with Maria. Helped Mum in the vegetable garden.

Saturday: Went to the market with Mum and Dad and helped buy food.

Ask them what they did with their leisure time. For example:

Monday: Played with Jenifa after school

Tuesday: Took the pet turtle some rice.

Wednesday: Went swimming with Maria and Pia. Played soccer with Simon and Kali.

Saturday: Went to town with Mum. Watched a video at Lani's house.

Sunday: Went to church. Played with cousins on the beach. Caught fish for turtle.

Students are to make a list of some things that they could do next week to help someone in their community.
Is there someone old who needs help?
Is there someone sick who needs help?
Is there someone who is kind to you who you could help?

Money

Provide coins for the students to examine.
Discuss the animals on the toea coins.

5t: turtle
10t: cuscus
20t: cassowary
50t: festivals
1K: crocodile

Talk about traditional money that is still in use today in PNG, such as tabu shell money from East New Britain and Bagi from Milne Bay Province.

Coin rubbings. Ask students to place a piece of paper over each coin and rub over it gently with the flat lead of a pencil. The picture on the coin will appear on the paper. Cut these out.

E Sit students in a circle on the floor with their paper money. Ask students to put their 'money' on the floor in front of them and then choose students to do sums.

For example: **Pekoia, can you make K1 using seven coins?**

Answer could be: **20t + 20t + 20t + 10t+ 10t +10t +10t.**

Other questions could be:

Which coins make 20t?
Which coins add up to K1.20?
How many 5t make K1?
How many 10t make K10?

Using fractions:
Find half (½) of one kina.
How much is a quarter (¼) of one kina?
How much is ¼ of 20 toea?
How much is ½ of 10 toea?

 Ask students to work out these money problems.

1 Sali bought four pawpaw. They cost K1.20 each. How much did she pay? (K4.80.)

2 Tali had K20. He bought a drink for K1.40, a pie for K2.20 and some chips for K3. How much change did he get? (K13.40.)

3 Jono had K15. He lost K6.80 when it fell out of his pocket. How much money did he have left? (K8.20.)

4 Simon wants to buy a bike. He is saving his pocket money in the bank. The bike costs K120 and he has K60. How much more money does he need to save? (K60.)

5 Tep has a job after school, working in the trade store for Jon and Ana. He works for one hour every day of the week and gets paid K4 an hour. How much money does he make a week? (K28.)

6 Letti and Lani sold some food at the market. They got K6 for bananas, K2 for a pineapple, K5 for some shells and K4.50 for some fresh fish. How much money did they make? (K17.50.)

7 Kali caught six tilapia. He sold them for K5 each at the market. He spent K10 on some sunglasses. How much money did he have left? (K20.)

Elizabeth and Kena own a PMV. They make about K350 a week.
Out of this money, they have to take out business expenses:

K75 for petrol

K10 for insurance

K20 for repairs

K5 for oil

The money they have left is called the **profit**.
Students are to work out how much profit Elizabeth and Kena make each week from their business.

(V) Talk about saving your money in the bank so that it can grow.
Get someone from the bank to come and talk to the students about saving their money.

 Students should learn these money words:

save, spend, interest, profit, buy, sell, cost.

A happy memory

A **happy memory** is when you remember a happy time that you had.
Having a **good memory** means that you can remember things easily.

 Study the **story map** with students and discuss.

Read the story aloud starting with the opening sentence.
It should be something like this:

I remember on my tenth birthday we went to Madang.

We stayed with our Aunty Molli and Uncle Poi.

I played on the beach with my two cousins, Susy and Ana, and we went swimming.

Later on, we had a mumu with my aunty and uncle and cousins and some wantoks who live in Madang.

That night, we all went to the movies to see King Kong. It was really scary, and I held on to Mum's hand in the scary parts of the movie.

For the next story, read through the suggestions for **when who where why what**.
Ask students to read the story, which should be something like this:

Last Thursday I went with Lani and James to the swimming hole at Lambui to play and swim. We swung on the vines and fell into the water.

It was great fun!

  Now ask students to make up their own story using **when who where why what**.

Choose students to read their stories to the rest of the class when they have finished.

Things we need

Students should study the picture. Ask students to choose things that we need.

Answers:

Things we need	Things we want
taps	television
water tank	truck, car
canoe	mobile phone
chairs	video camera
bed	motorbike
rubbish bin	football
bilum	helicopter
knife	swimming pool
food	fishing boat
clothes	bicycle
toothbrush	handbag
comb	sunglasses

How many of these words can students find in the picture of **Things we need**?

Students should make a list of things that they want and would buy if they had the money.

Students can cut out pictures of things in magazines and put them in two columns. One column should be headed **Things I need** and the other should be headed **Things I want**.

E Ask students to think about the important things that they have at home. Get them to list them and then draw them.

E Ask students to draw pictures of things that they have seen in the shops and would like to buy. These would be things that they **want**.

Shopping

E Students are to form pairs and role-play a conversation between a shop assistant and a customer.

Shop assistant: Good morning! Can I help you?

Customer: Good morning! How much are these shorts?

Shop assistant: They are K20. Would you like to try them on?

Customer: Yes, thank you.

Shop assistant: That's a good fit on you!

Customer: Yes! I'll take them please.

E Students should think up some other conversations about shopping and role-play these.

Phrases to use:

How much is ....?

How much are ....?

Can I try this on?

Can I have this please?

Do you have any ....?

Does this come in a bigger size?

READER 3: Shopping For Shoes: A Play

Read the play through first, then choose students to be the characters. For this play you will need eleven pairs of shoes. If you can't get these, just use two pairs, pretending they are different ones each time they are used.

New vocabulary: **special**, **window**, **size**, **think**, **tight**, **loose**, **laces**, **straps**, **plenty**, **light**, **heavy**, **cost**.

What does **window shopping** mean? (It means that you are just looking at goods but not intending to buy anything.)

Students should find, in the text, the opposites to these words: bigger (smaller), tight (loose), light (heavy).

Work out how much the shoes cost altogether. (K18.50.)

Mum gave Rina K20. How much change did she get? (K1.50.)

Advertising

Answers:
Write down the adjectives in this advertisement. **Cool, sweet, delicious, creamy, mouth-watering.**
Write down the words that make you want to eat this ice cream. **Sweet, delicious, creamy, mouth-watering.**
What is the brand name of this ice cream? **Sugarice.**
Why did they choose this name? **It sounds sweet and cold.**

Direct students to make up their own drink. They could use oranges, lemons, watermelon, coconut milk or mangoes. Write down the recipe:
For example:

Tropical Delight

2 oranges	Squeeze the juice from the oranges and lemon into a jar.
1 lemon	Scoop the pulp out of the passionfruit.
1 passionfruit	Add the other ingredients to the jar and shake it.
1 tbsp sugar	Pour into a glass with ice.
1 cup water.	Decorate with a flower at the top of the glass.

Students must make up an ad for their drink.
They should think up a brand name and some good adjectives like **fruity**, **smooth**, **thick**, **creamy**.

 They should draw a picture of their ad.

E Small groups of four or five students should make up a **jingle** (a catchy song) to advertise their drink on the radio or TV.
They should practise it outside and then sing it to the class.
Use sounds to go with it; for example, gurgling sounds, popping sounds, fizzing sounds, pouring water sounds, clinking ice sounds, gulping sounds.

E Students could advertise a **drink stand** and set one up at lunchtime at school to sell their drinks to the students for 50t each.
They could make posters to advertise the drinks and sing their jingles.
The drinks could be put in clean bottles labelled with the brand name or sold in plastic glasses.

E Students can look in **magazines** for advertisements. They should cut them out and glue them into their books. Then they should answer the questions in the Student Book about each advertisement.

Trading

  Talk about trading things of equal value.

E Discuss the pictures and decide which things would be worth trading.
The sentences below are only examples.

1 A **knife** could be worth a necklace and a kina shell.

2 The **four Bird of Paradise feathers** could be worth a shell necklace.

3 The **kina shell** could be worth the shell necklace and a pineapple and four Bird of Paradise feathers.

4 A **fish** could be worth six oranges and a pineapple.

Organise a **barter party**. Students should bring some things to school to trade. They could bring things like:

shells, pocket-knife, necklace, feathers, spear, hat, pen, rubber, fruit, comb, bilum, mat, sunglasses, soap, mumu, mangoes, books.

Students have to move around the classroom and decide what they will trade their items for. They must decide what they think their items are worth compared to things other people want to trade. If they cannot decide, they can ask the teacher to decide whether it is a fair trade.

E After the barter party, students should write down the things that they traded and what they traded them for.

V Talk about things that are **valuable** to different cultures.
Today, money is valuable to all societies, but what traditional things were valuable to us in the past?
Discuss things like **pigs**, **kina shells**, **bagi** or **dog's teeth (necklaces)**.
What traditional things are considered valuable in your community today?

V Ask students to discuss this topic.

V Students are to write about something that their family has that is of **traditional value**. For example, it may be a kina shell, a hagen axe, or ceremonial bilas.

Traditional trading

V Discuss the Kula trade. Do students know any more about it? Find out more information on the internet or from books in the library.

Words that don't belong:

stone head water

Traditional penalties

In some parts of PNG, if village laws are broken, people must still pay traditional penalties. For example, to stop people from over-fishing in certain areas, village law stops people from taking their canoes into these areas.
In some villages, if people are caught, they have to pay:

1 pig   1 param shell money   K20   garden food.

Students could draw these and discuss local penalties.

The Kula trade

  Read this to the students.

How the bagi (necklaces) are made

First, the men dive for Chama shells (rock oysters).

Next, the shells are broken into small pieces.

The pink pieces of the shell are made smaller with hammers.

These small pieces are hammered again into tiny pieces.

Then these pieces are polished smooth.

They are ground on a stone using sand and water until they are round and thin.

Next, holes are made in them using hand drills.

Finally, they are strung onto string made from pandanus root.

There are 150 to 200 discs on each necklace.

These are ground again so that they are all the same size.

To turn a common bagi into an important Kula piece, the necklace must be 6 to 15 feet long.

Ask the children to repeat this process to you.
Ask questions like:

What happened next?

What was the last thing they did?

How did they make common bagi into Kula bagi?

Find pictures of these and draw them.

The Hiri trade

Talk about the Hiri trade between the Motuans of Central Province and the Gulf people. The Motuans took their clay pots in outrigger canoes called Lakatois and exchanged these pots with the Gulf people for sago. To remember this trade, the Hiri Moale Festival is held each year.

Teaching English

Note the use of these adjectives:

small   smaller   tiny

Silent letters

Some letters in words are silent. You cannot hear their sound when saying the word. Look at these words and say them:

Silent **b**:	com**b**	lim**b** (leg)	tom**b** (grave)	clim**b**
Silent **k**:	**k**nife	**k**nee	**k**not	**k**now

Moka pig exchange

E Find out more information about this ceremony on the internet or from books in the library. Write down what you find out about it.

Read this text to the students and discuss.

The Highlanders killed pigs in ceremonies where one clan gave the pigs to another clan. After some years, the clan who received the pigs then paid them back with extra pigs. This was like an investment.

Sometimes live pigs, snakes and cassowaries were exchanged as well.

Today, this Moka ceremony also includes cash or money, and goods from stores.

Discuss **Highland neck adornments**. These are strips of short bamboo slats that hang from the neck. Each strip represents a number of gold-lipped pearl oyster shells (kina shells) that have been given away. The longer the length, the greater the wealth. Wealth is measured by how much you give away.

Students could make a Highland neck adornment by cutting small pieces of wood to the same length and then tying them together with string or twine down each side so it looks like a small ladder.

READER 4: Fun at the Pigsty

Read the story with the students.

New vocabulary: **rolled**, **crashed**, **followed**, **gate**, **sty**, **squeal**, **catch**, **caught**, **towards**, **chased**.

Why did they call the big fat pig Porky?

What is pig meat called? (Pork.)

What did Sela and Bili feed the pigs?

What else would they feed them?

Why did Sela and Bili apologise to Laena?

What do you think they said?

At the market

Study the pictures of the market with students. Is this market in the Highlands or by the coast? Why?

Students should look at the picture and make a list of the things that people have made to sell at the market. (Carvings, mats baskets, bilums.) Draw them.

 Students should think of some things that they could make to sell at the market, and draw them.

Students are to pretend that their mother is sick and they have to buy food at the market for their family for the week. They should make a shopping list so that they have a balanced diet for the week.

  How could your local marketplace be improved?

Students are to draw their ideas and write a paragraph explaining what could be done.

Students should find out who maintains their local market.

Teaching English

Look at the market pictures and add **ing** to the verbs.

Revise the rules for adding **ing** to words.

1. When a verb ends in **e**, drop the **e** before adding **ing**.

   e.g. **waste** becomes **wasting**
   share becomes **sharing**

2. When a verb ends in a consonant, double the consonant before adding **ing**.

   e.g. **drip** becomes **dripping**
   swim becomes **swimming**

3. If the verb contains two vowels, then just add **ing**.

   e.g. **leak** becomes **leaking**
   eat becomes **eating**

Students should study the market picture and put the things for sale into the right column.

Answers:

Vegetables	Fruit	Sea products	Animal products	Handcrafts
kaukau	bananas	fish	eggs	bilums
kumu	pawpaw	crabs	piglets	mats
taro	pineapple	shells	meat	baskets
pitpit	watermelon	shellfish	chickens	carvings
breadfruit	oranges			shell beads
pumpkin	coconut			anklets
peanuts	sugar cane			leis
	passionfruit			

Answers:

1. The man is **spitting** betel nut juice on the ground.
2. The child is **licking** an ice block.
3. The dog is **sniffing** the rubbish.
4. The baby on its mother's back is **crying**.
5. The small pig is **squealing** and **pulling** its leg, trying to get free.
6. The chickens are **flapping** their wings.
7. The girl is **eating** a banana.
8. The children are **drinking** Coca-Cola.
9. The man is **smoking** a cigarette.
10. The woman is **weaving** a mat.

Bingo

How to make a bingo game

Make a list of words to do with a particular topic. For example:

At the market

sell	buy	toea
kina	money	fruit
vegetables	tables	carvings
handcrafts	basket	bilum
shells	meat	fish

Using recycled cardboard, make a set of six cards. Rule up each card into nine squares and write one of the topic words in each square. For example:

money	fruit	kina
meat	**shells**	**buy**
sell	**fish**	**toea**

Write a different assortment of these words on each card. For example:

Card 1: basket, fruit, fish, meat, tables, kina, buy, bilum, sell.

Card 2: handcrafts, basket, carvings, shells, vegetables, meat, fish, toea, buy.

Card 3: sell, tables, shells, fish, buy, basket, meat, kina, toea.

When you have filled the six big cards, you must then write out each word on single cards on small squares of cardboard, like this:

There must be six small cards for each word on the list.

How to play bingo

1. Choose a group of six students to play. They sit in a circle with their bingo card in front of them.
2. All the single small cards sit on the floor in the middle of the circle.
3. Another student calls out one of the words and the others must look to see if that word is on their card. If it is, they must find the single card with that word written on it and put it on top of that word on their card.
4. The game continues like this, until someone fills up their whole card. They shout BINGO and win the game.
5. Keep all the cards in a recycled box so they don't get lost, with the name of the topic written on the lid.
6. Choose other topic words from the workbook to make other bingo sets. This game can be played when students finish other work.

Looking after other places in the community

  Ask students to list things in the community that everyone uses.

These could be:

Local airstrip, football field, village square, village haus wind, church, marketplace, roads, swimming hole, water tanks.

Ask students who maintains these places. If they don't know then they must find out. What kind of maintenance do they require?

Make up a **table** like this and ask students to fill it in.

Airstrip	Church	Market	Football field	Village square	Haus wind
weeding	painting	painting	mowing	weeding	repairing roof
cutting grass	cleaning	repairing roof/tables	clearing away stones	sweeping	putting in rubbish bins
	looking after gardens	picking up rubbish	picking up rubbish	looking after flower gardens	

If we help to do these things for the community, should we get paid? Why not?

E Read this story to the class and then discuss the questions underneath.

In 1970 there was a drought in the Highlands. The people had no food, so the Australian government said it would help. They asked the local people to clear the land near their villages to make an airstrip so they could fly in supplies.

The people worked hard and made an airstrip. Soon a plane flew in and landed on the airstrip. It had tinned meat and rice for the people. They did not have to pay for it.

The people got the food and then they asked to be paid for building the airstrip.

1 Do you think the people should have been paid for building the airstrip? Why not?
2 Did Australia ask to be paid for the food? Did they have to give it to the people for free?
3 What do you think the saying 'give and take' means?
4 Should we do things to help our community for nothing?

Traditional counting

V E Look at the diagram and count this way with the students.

Students are to draw a whole body and count up to 50 using body parts. Then they should count by 2's and 5's to 50 using the same system.

Cargo cults

V Discuss the text and picture. KWL what students know about cargo cults.

Answers:

1 People can only get goods if they first pay **money** for them.
2 The goods are then sent to the people by **plane**.
3 Everyone has to **work** to get money.
4 Then they can **buy** goods.

  Read the following story about the **cargo cult** and discuss.

In the 1970s there was a Baining cargo cult leader named Melki who taught that a bomb would drop on New Britain killing everyone except the Bainings (people who live in New Britain).

After that, a giant egg would arrive full of cargo that was to be shared among the people.

They believed that when this happened there would be enough 'cargo' for everyone to live happily and never have to work again.

To make sure that his followers kept on believing him, Melki took them up to the top of Mt Sinivit where the Bainings believed a female goddess named Namugi lived.

To impress the people, Melki spoke to the goddess and told the people that he also had the power to arrange earthquakes and storms.

Many people believed these things, but they are still waiting for the cargo to arrive.

  Ask for students' opinions on cargo cults.

Me and my Responsibilities

Learning outcomes

Topic: Community living

4.1.2 Explain behaviour that promotes good relationships in the wider community.
4.1.3 Evaluate community services and the roles and responsibilities related to them.
4.2.1 Describe ways goods and services are exchanged in the community.
4.3.1 Describe customs related to events of significance.

Topic: Environmental studies

4.1.2 Describe the impact of changes to the environment and identify solutions to potentially harmful changes.

Topic: Art and craft

Posters.

Topic: Drama

Play: Reader 7: The Brave Hunters.

Topic: Sport

Outdoor games.

Topic: Mathematics

Game: Addition/subtraction.

Unit summary

Topics	Pictures and oral discussion	Student Book activities	Teacher Book activities	Cross-curriculum objectives	Language objectives
My responsibilities	Discuss personal responsibilities.	Choose correct responses.		Community living 4.1.2	Discussion 4.1.2 V
My responsibilities at home	Discuss.	Put words in correct order. Choose correct words. Lists.		Community living 4.1.2	Correct order 4.1.2 E
My responsibilities to my pet	Discuss caring for a pet.	Choose correct words. Pet diary.	Draw and write about pet. Graph. Interviews. Poem. Big Book.	Community living 4.1.2	Diary. Poem 4.3.1 E
Reader 5: Maria's Puppy	Read story.		New vocabulary. Answer questions about story.	Community living	4.1.2 E 4.2.1 E
Keeping the home safe	Discuss newspaper report.	Make list.		Community living	Making lists.
Posters	Discuss poster.	Make a poster.		Art: Posters	4.3.1 E
My responsibilities to my community	Discuss responsibilities.	Opinion. Adjectives. Ideas.	Write about responsibilities.	Community living	Adjectives. Opinions. 4.1.2 V 4.1.4 E
Reader 6: Amo's Story	Read story together.		New vocabulary. Answer questions about story Debate.	Community living	4.2.1 E
Respecting others	Discuss.	Draw cartoon. Finish speech bubble.	Speech marks.	Culture Community living 4.1.2	Opinions. Adjectives. 4.1.4 E 4.3.1 E

Me and my Responsibilities

Topics	Pictures and oral discussion	Student Book activities	Teacher Book activities	Cross-curriculum objectives	Language objectives
Good manners (customs)	Discuss good manners and customs.	Choose correct answers. Write about customs.		Culture 4.1.2	Choosing. 4.1.2 E
Fighting with your friends	Discuss.	Finish writing sentences. Who was right?		Community living Personal growth.	Words that don't belong.
Reader 7: The Brave Hunters: A Play	Read story together.		New vocabulary. Answer questions about story. Hunting rules. Opinions. Make up song. Plurals. Compound words.	Gender	4.1.1 V 4.2.1 E 4.3.3 V
Conflict in the village	Discuss pictures.	Give opinions.	Jumping to conclusions. Persuasive language. Differing points of view.	Community living	Opinions.
Cassowary races	Discuss.	Give opinions.		Community living 4.3.1	Opinions. 4.1.2 V
Payback	Discuss.	Give opinions.		Culture Community living 4.3.1	Opinions. 4.1.2 V 4.1.4 E
Making up with your friends	Discuss pictures.	Write letter of apology.	Discuss experiences of conflict.	Personal growth. 4.2.1	Letters. 4.3.3 V
Apologising	Discuss.	Write in speech bubbles. Write letter of apology.	Phrases.	Personal growth. 4.2.1	4.3.1 E 4.1.2 E

Me and my Responsibilities

Me and my Responsibilities

Topics	Pictures and oral discussion	Student Book activities	Teacher Book activities	Cross-curriculum objectives	Language objectives
Compromising	Discuss.	Write correct endings to sentences.	Making compromises.	Personal growth. 4.2.1	Choosing endings. 4.3.2 E
Helping people in trouble	Discuss.	Choose best answers.		Personal growth. 4.2.1	Choosing.
Reader 8: The Working Bee	Read story together.		New vocabulary. Answer questions about story. Colour in.	Community living 4.1.3	E
My responsibilities to my village	Discuss picture.	Finish sentences. Verbs. Nouns. Past tense.	Adjectives. Opposites. Is or are. Lists. Who/what.	Community living 4.1.3	Finish sentences. Nouns. Verbs. Past tense. 4.3.2 E
My responsibilities to my school	Study pictures.	Find things wrong in pictures. Diagrams. Safety.	Fix things. Design diagrams. Before/after. Design poster.	Community living. Posters.	Choose correct sentences.
Using our time wisely	Discuss.	Fill in time line.		Personal growth.	
Legends	Discuss purpose of legends.		Read two legends. Activities.	Outdoor games.	Legends. Retelling.
How responsible are you?	Discuss rules of game.	Play game.		Mathematics + −	Following instructions.
Our country	Discuss questions.	Answer questions. Draw flag.		Map work.	National anthem.

My responsibilities

V Discuss what the students feel to be their responsibilities in the home.

Answers:

Telling the truth
Being sensible
Going to school
Helping others
Being loyal to your family
Being tidy
Helping at home

My responsibilities at home

Answers:

1 We should help our family.
2 We should help our grandparents.
3 We should be kind to each other.
4 We should share our food.
5 We should share the work in the house.

My responsibilities to my family

Answers:

1 We need to help our parents by doing **chores**.
2 We need to help our younger brothers and **sisters**.
3 We need to help our **grandparents**.
4 We need to help in the **vegetable** garden.
5 We need to look after family members when they are **sick**.
6 We need to **obey** our parents.
7 We need to be **tidy** in the home.
8 We need to keep ourselves **clean**.
9 We need to look after our **clothes** and shoes.

Answers:

dirty: **clean**
untidy: **tidy**
disobey: **obey**
healthy: **sick**
fast: **slow**
take: **give**
happy: **angry**

My responsibilities to my pet

Answers:

1 You must make it a **home** or a bed.
2 You must give it fresh **water** every day.
3 You must give it **food** every day.
4 You must exercise it if it's a **dog**.
5 You must **wash** your dog when it's dirty.

Things that a dog can eat:

meat	bones	dog biscuits	kaukau
fish	taro	food scraps	bread

READER 5: Maria's Puppy

Read through the story with the students.

New vocabulary: **puppies**, **promise**, **chose**, **black**, **white**, **Boots**, **basket**, **warm**, **sniffed**, **bowl**, **scraps**, **cute**, **toy**, **patted**, **eaten**, **glad**.

What things did Maria have to do to look after her puppy?

What did he need every day?

What do puppies like to do most?

How did this get Boots into trouble?

Is it easy having a pet? Why/why not?

Why was Pia glad that Boots was Maria's pet and not hers?

Ask which students have pets.
KWL some animals that could be kept as pets; for example, dogs, cats, turtles, cuscus, cassowary, mice, guinea pigs.
Students who do not have a pet should choose one of the above and pretend that animal is their pet.

Students must make a pet diary, using the one in the Student Book as a guide. They should write down everything they would do in one week to look after their pet. Students who do not have a real pet should write about their imaginary pet.

Students must draw their pet and write three sentences about it.
For example:

My pet is a lizard. Its name is Zoro. It eats small insects.

Draw a sample graph on the blackboard and ask students to copy it into their books. They should fill it in by asking others in the class what kind of pet they have.
For example:

Cat	Dog	Mouse	Turtle	Cuscus	Guinea pig	Parrot	Frog
	Stu						
Sala	Alex						
Mia	Peggy	Meg		Ben		Ama	
John	James	Anis	Letti	Jack	Joshua	Angon	Peter

When students have filled in their own graphs from their research, fill in the graph on the blackboard as a class. Find out which students filled in their graph correctly.
This could also be filled in as a pictograph, where students draw a picture of each pet.

Students must find out about three other people's pets by interviewing other students. They must do this by asking questions like:

What is your pet's name?

What does it look like?

Where did you find it?

What does he eat?

Where does he sleep?

What does he like to do?

They must write a brief description of the three pets. For example:

Angon's Parrot

Angon's parrot is red, green and blue.
He found it in the bush with a sore wing.
It eats seeds and berries.

Jack's Cuscus

Jack's cuscus is called Scratch.
He sleeps in an old sock.
He likes eating bananas and climbing up Jack's pants.

Mia's Kitten

Mia's kitten is called Princess.
She is black and white.
She sleeps in a shoebox.

Students are to form small groups and read out their sentences to each other.
Students are to write a poem about their pet.
It could be something like this:

My Frog

My frog, Kung Fu, is slimy and green,
He's the meanest frog you've ever seen.
He lives in a rock pool out by my shed,
He croaks "nidip" whenever he's fed.

Make a Big Book with these pet poems and have students draw large pictures to go with their poems.

Keeping the home safe

Things in the home that are dangerous:

Medicines: these should be kept in a safe place. They should only be taken as recommended by the doctor.

Matches: these should be kept out of the reach of small children.

Cleaners: these should be kept out of the reach of young children.

Petrol: this should be kept in a tin away from the house.

Kerosene: this should be kept in a tin or bottle in a safe place.

Insect spray: this should be used carefully and kept away from young children.

Students are to make a safety poster about using matches. The poster should follow the guidelines given in the Student Book. You can display the best posters around the classroom.

My responsibilities to my community

Answer:
Kali should help Amo clean the fish, because Amo would share the fish with them and it would be Kali's dinner. It is his responsibility to help.

E Ask students to write about what they think are their responsibilities towards their community. When finished, they should share their ideas with the class.

READER 6: Amo's Story

Read the story together.

New vocabulary: **elder**, **life**, **changes**, **fifty**, **officer**, **tribal fighting**, **fought**, **trouble**, **settle**, **leave**, **often**, **cartoons**, **laugh**.

What changes in the community does Amo think are good?

What changes does Amo think are bad?

What do you think about this?

What changes do you think are good and bad?

Do you respect the older people in your community?

Do you ask them for their opinions?

Do you think they know more than you do?

V **Debate** about TV and video games. Are they good or bad? Is it good to watch violent TV shows? Is it good to play violent video games? Is it good to watch funny cartoons that make you laugh?

Me and my Responsibilities

Respecting others

Teaching English

Speech marks

When people talk in a story, we use speech marks to tell us what they say. Ask students to put the words in speech bubbles into sentences with speech marks.

"Look, that man's got a huge bandage on his head!" said Simon.

"He looks really stupid!" said Kali.

"Don't make fun of him. That's what they wear in India," said Letti.

"It's called a turban."

"Amo is too old to be a village elder!" said Simon.

"Yeah! He's always talking and telling us how to do things!" said Kali.

"You need to show respect to your elders!" said Dad. "Amo knows a lot more about life than you two young pups!"

Good manners (customs)

Answers:
If you are at a birthday party at your friend's house, and there is lots of food on the table, what should you do? **Wait until you are told to eat. Do not push in to get food. Wait until there is room to get to the table.**
If a stranger holds out his hand to you, what should you do? **Shake his hand.**
If you are walking in front of a visitor at your school and you both want to go into the classroom, what should you do? **Open the door for the visitor to walk into the classroom first.**
If people are in a line, waiting to buy something, what should you do? **Wait behind the last person in line.**
You are travelling on a PMV and an old woman gets on. You are sitting down but there is no seat for her. What should you do? **Get up and let her sit in your seat.**

Me and my Responsibilities

Fighting with your friends

Answer:
No one was right and no one was wrong in this situation.

READER 7: The Brave Hunters: A Play

Read through the story.

New vocabulary: **hunting**, **brave**, **knife**, **hiding**, **grunt**, **shoot**, **squealing**, **except**, **others**, **waiting**, **giant**, **charges**, **trips**, **all right**.

Choose characters to be in the play.

Act out the play with props. (Bow and arrow, spear, knife, stick.)

Talk about whether girls are as brave as boys.

Can girls do the same things that boys can do?

Should we discriminate like this?

Students are to write about a time when they went hunting.

V Many people have been accidentally shot in hunting accidents. Talk about hunting rules that should be followed to prevent such accidents.

V Have a **debate** about whether guns or traditional weapons should be used for hunting. Students must be able to give reasons for their opinion.

E Here is a Maori song (in English) about hunting rabbits. Teach it to the students. Make up your own tune.

Run rabbit! Run rabbit! Run, run, run.
Run rabbit! Run rabbit! Run, run, run.
Bang! Bang! Bang! He missed!
Went the farmer's gun.
Run rabbit! Run rabbit! Run, run, run!

In small groups, students can make up their own hunting songs by changing some of the words. For example:

Fly pigeon! Fly pigeon! Fly, fly, fly.
Fly pigeon! Fly pigeon! Fly, fly, fly.
Bang! Bang! Bang! He missed!
Went the hunter's gun.
Fly pigeon! Fly pigeon! Fly, fly, fly!

Make up actions to go with it.

Teaching English

Compound words

Teach students about compound words.

Find two smaller words in these words:

classroom	birthday	bandage	blackboard	grandparent	something
playground	outdoor	roadside	outside	sandpit	newspaper

Plurals

We change '**f**' to '**v**' before adding '**es**'.

knife – **knives**   calf – **calves**   half – **halves**

Conflict in the village

Possible answers:

V Talk about how people often **jump to conclusions** (believe something that isn't true) simply because someone suggests that it could have happened.
Talk about how important it is to have all the **facts** before you accuse people of wrongdoing. There was no **proof** that Miti took the piglet.

E Sometimes people use **persuasive** language to persuade you to believe something. It could be something that is true or something that isn't really true.

> "I saw Miti over by the piggery watching the pigs last Sunday when he came to visit his aunty. He looked very interested in them. I'm sure that he was looking at the piglets and thinking about how he could easily take one back to his village without anyone seeing him. I'm sure that he stole the piglet," said Peta.

 Explain to the class that this was only Peta's **point of view**. It does not prove that Miti took the piglet.

Discuss the students' **points of view**.

Scenario: A child runs across the road chasing a dog and a big truck screeches to a halt. All its cargo falls off onto the road, which kills the dog and injures the boy.

The people who were watching were Kira (the village policeman), Elizabeth, James and Mrs Pedu.

They all saw the same thing but had different points of view about what happened.

Here is what they said:

It wasn't the driver's fault. The boy suddenly ran out onto the road in front of him!

Elizabeth

The truck driver was going way too fast in a built up area. His cargo wasn't tied on properly and he should have been driving slower!

Kira

The boy was chasing his dog and the dog was chasing a ball. The boy didn't even see the truck!

James

Children should be taught to be careful on a busy road. He should have looked first!

Mrs Pedu

Whose fault was the accident?

Making up with your friends

Students could write a letter like this:

Dear Letti,

I'm very sorry that I took your book without asking you and I'm sorry for lying to you.

Please forgive me, as I want you to still be my friend.

I won't steal from you again.

Your friend,

Lani

Discussion. It can sometimes be very hard to admit that we are wrong. Some people find it very hard to **apologise**. If we can say sorry, we can be forgiven for what we have done wrong and the conflict comes to an end. If we do not say sorry, the conflict continues and we may even lose a friend.
Ask students for their experiences. What do they think?

Me and my Responsibilities

Apologising

Answers should be something like these:

Teaching English

Teach students other phrases to use when saying sorry. Students should practise saying these to each other in pairs.

I'm sorry about that!

I'm sorry for not .... (calling you!)

Forgive me!

It was my fault! I'm sorry.

I didn't mean to .... (hurt you.)

It was silly of me to .... (throw a stone.)

Compromising

Answers:
Simon wanted to call **the team the Tigers.**
Anis thought it was a stupid name because **he thought it should be a PNG name.**
He suggested that the team **should be called the Cassowaries.**
James thought that name **was no good because it was too long.**
John suggested they call themselves **the Eagles.**
Tom thought that was **a good idea because there are eagles in PNG.**
Danni agreed because **eagles fly fast and they are hunters.**
This is called **compromising.**

Answers:
Your friend wants to go to see a movie on Saturday, but you want to go swimming at the beach.
A compromise: You could say to your friend that you could go swimming in the morning and go to the movies in the afternoon.
Mum wants you to dig a hole to bury some rubbish after school, but you have football practice.
A compromise: You could promise to dig the hole as soon as you came home from football practice.
Dad wants help with making a new fence, but you want to go and play in the river with your friends.
A compromise: You could help Dad with the fence first and then go and play in the river with your friends, or play with them tomorrow.

Helping people in trouble

Answers (any or all of the answers given):

Laena has hurt her leg. She can't walk. She has to get her vegetables to the market to sell them. What could you do to help?

Tell her you're very sorry that she's not well.

Get a friend to help you and take her vegetables to market and sell them for her.

Go and ask her if you can help in any way.

Amo needs some bush rope to fix his outrigger canoe. He has no money and the bush rope is far away up in the hills. What could you do to help?

Go into the bush to get some bush rope for him.

Get someone to take him up to the hills in their truck so he can cut some bush rope.

Ana has just had a call to say that Jon has had a car accident. She has to go to see him in hospital. What could you do to help?

Offer to look after the trade store while she's away.

Tell her that you hope Jon is all right.

The fence on Bili's pigsty has been broken by a bad storm and some of the pigs have escaped into the bush. What could you do to help?

Help him to fix the fence.

Chase the pigs that ran away and help catch them.

Kena's PMV won't start. Elizabeth is sick and he has to take her to hospital. What could you do to help?

Find Dad and ask him to help fix the PMV.

Ask Mum to look at Elizabeth.

Offer to look after their small children.

Pastor John is organising a working bee at the church to do repairs. What could you do to help?

Clean inside the church.

Weed the gardens around the church.

Pick some flowers for the church.

READER 8: The Working Bee

Read the story with the students.

New vocabulary: **lovely**, **hardest**, **deserve**, **chocolate**, **supposed**, **another**, **arrived**, **mixed**, **trouble**, **promised**.

What day of the week do you think it was? Why?

What jobs were other people doing at the working bee?

Can you get paint out of your hair easily?

Why did the girls say the boys looked like old men?

Explain that '**can I give you a hand**' means 'can I help you'.

A **working bee** means that everyone helps to do something for the community without getting paid.

Colour in the pictures, using a red pencil to show the red paint in the girls' hair.

My responsibilities to my village

Answers could be something like these:

1. Letti is sweeping the path around the **houses**.
2. Dad is fixing Kena's PMV so that **he can transport people**.
3. Peta and Bili are putting new metal **on the road**.
4. Maria and Elizabeth are planting hibiscus bushes **along the path**.
5. Amo and Simon are fixing the **fences around the gardens**.
6. Kira and Pastor John are painting the **church**.
7. Mum and Aunty Meri are weaving new **thatch** for the house.
8. Laena is weeding the **garden**.
9. Sam and Grace are burning the **rubbish**.
10. Rina and Jimi are chasing a **pig**.

Teaching English

Adjectives

Students are to match these **adjectives** with the nouns in the table below.

dusty (road)	wooden (fence)
smelly (rubbish)	colourful (hibiscus)
white (church)	stony (path)
winding (pathway)	crowded (PMV)
greedy (pig)	fertile (garden)

Opposites

Students are to find the opposites to these words.

breaking (fixing)	dirty (clean)
straight (winding)	old (new)
bad (good)	happy (sad)
win (lose)	safe (unsafe)
cut (uncut)	

Nouns	Present tense verbs	Past tense verbs
paths houses	sweeping	swept
PMV	fixing	fixed
metal road	putting	put
hibiscus bushes pathway	planting	planted
fences gardens	fixing	fixed
church	painting	painted
thatch roof	weaving	wove
garden	weeding	weeded
rubbish	burning	burnt
pig	chasing	chased

Some of these will be different depending on how students finished the sentences.

Me and my Responsibilities

Me and my Responsibilities

Singular and plural

Talk to students about using **is** (singular) or **are** (plural).

We **are** painting the fence.

He **is** painting the fence.

Students need to choose **is** or **are** in the following examples.

1 They **are** chasing the pigs.

2 She **is** burning the rubbish.

3 They **are** fixing the fence.

4 Maria **is** sweeping the path.

5 Laena **is** weeding the garden.

6 Rina and Jimi **are** driving to town.

7 He **is** painting the church.

8 Dad **is** fixing the PMV.

Students are to write a **list** of things that could be done around their village. They should pair up with students from the same village and organise a working bee. They can approach the village elder or chief and ask if they can do these things to improve the village.

E Ask the class the following questions in English. Students must look at the illustration on pages 58–9 of the Student Book for the answers and give their answers in English.

Who?

1 Who is putting new metal on the road? **Uncle Peta and Bili.**

2 Who is chasing a pig? **Rina and Jimi.**

3 Who is sweeping the path? **Letti.**

4 Who is burning the rubbish? **Uncle Sam and Aunty Grace.**

5 Who is fixing Kena's PMV? **Dad.**

6 Who is weeding the garden? **Laena.**

7 Who is planting hibiscus bushes? **Maria and Elizabeth.**

8 Who is fixing the fence? **Amo and Simon.**

9 Who is painting the church? **Pastor John and Kira.**

10 Who is weaving the new church roof? **Mum and Aunty Meri.**

What?

1 What are Mum and Aunty Meri doing? **Weaving a new roof.**

2 What are Pastor John and Kira doing? **Painting the church.**

3 What are Amo and Simon doing? **Fixing the fence.**

4 What are Elizabeth and Maria doing? **Planting hibiscus.**

5 What is Laena doing? **Weeding the garden.**

6 What is Dad doing? **Fixing Kena's PMV.**

7 What are Uncle Sam and Aunty Grace doing? **Burning the rubbish.**

8 What is Letti doing? **Sweeping the path.**

9 What are Rina and Jimi doing? **Chasing a pig.**

10 What are Uncle Peta and Bili doing? **Putting new metal on the road.**

My responsibilities to my school

These are all the things that are **wrong** in the picture.

1 The water tank has the tap running.

2 There is rubbish outside the toilet block.

3 There is a broken bottle in the playground.

4 A branch has fallen from the tree.

5 The uncut grassy area could have snakes.

6 The road outside the school does not have a pedestrian crossing and there is no teacher on duty. Children are crossing the road as a car is coming

7 There is broken spouting on the roof.

8 One classroom has a broken window.

9 There is a hole in the wall.

10 Boys are throwing stones at each other.

11 Children are fighting with sticks.

12 The ground is uneven and has potholes.

13 There is a broken seat outside the classroom.

These could be **fixed** by doing the following:
(These are suggestions only as the students may have other ideas.)

1 Put a sign by the tap saying '**Turn it off!**'

2 Put more rubbish bins around the school.

3 As above.

4 Remove broken branches from the school.

5 Have the students or caretaker cut the grass.

6 Paint a pedestrian crossing on the road (if sealed). A teacher should be on duty when students cross the road before and after school.

7 Fix the spouting.

8 Put tape on the window and get it fixed.

9 Repair the hole with bamboo or plywood.

10 Make a school rule about not throwing stones.

11 Make a school rule about not fighting/playing with sticks.

12 Fill the uneven ground with dirt.

13 Fix the broken seat.

Students are to draw a diagram like this.

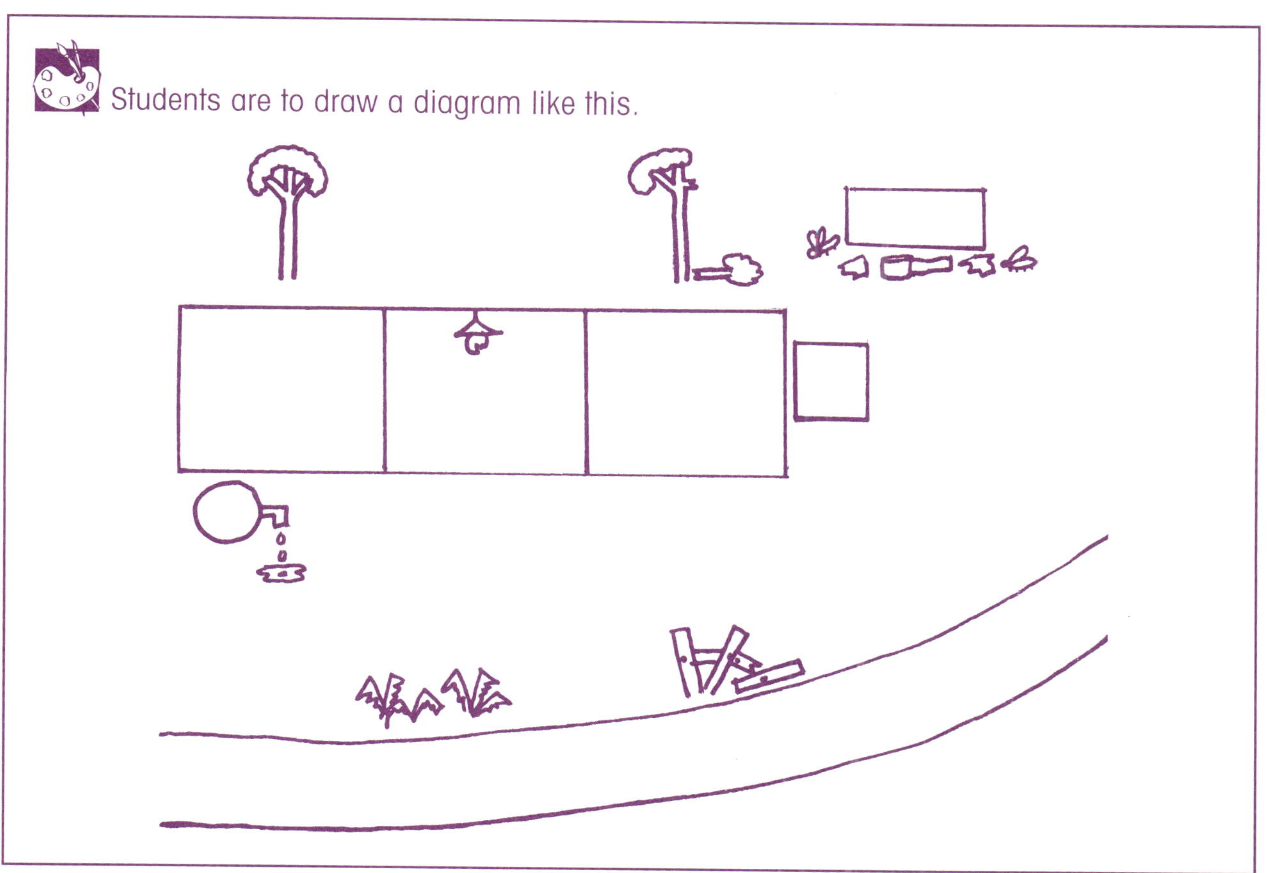

Students are to do the following activities, using diagrams where necessary:

Design an outdoor seat.

Design a swing.

Design a flower garden, naming the plants.

Design posters to put in the toilets.

Design a symbol or motto for the school.

Design a sign with the name of the school on it.

Design a road safety sign to go on the roadside outside the school.

Design a bell using an old wheel rim or something metallic.

Write a motto for the school.

Make up a song for the school.

Make up a 'cheer' for the school. This cheer could be used to encourage players on the sports field. Cheerleaders could make up a routine (dance) to go with the cheer.

Students could put in the rubbish bin, shade trees, fence and sandpit like this:

Some other things they could add to their school diagram are:

new seats new desks jungle gym vegetable garden

Correct sentences:

1 If we run around in the classroom, we might break the furniture.

2 We must not throw stones at other people in case someone gets hurt.

3 I always put rubbish in the rubbish bin.

4 We need to sit under shady trees to have our lunch.

5 We need to cut the grass around the school to keep snakes away.

6 We must keep the toilets clean and wash our hands.

7 Sticks can poke out someone's eye and make them blind.

8 We must always turn off the tap after drinking water.

9 I always look for cars before I cross the road.

10 It's not safe to play on fallen branches.

Teaching English

Using before and after

Have students complete the following sentences.

1 Turn out the light .... going to sleep.

2 Wash your hands .... eating lunch.

3 Wash your hands .... using the toilet.

4 Always look .... crossing the road.

5 Clean your teeth .... you eat.

6 You must learn English .... you can be a teacher.

7 You should not swim .... a meal.

8 You need to learn the rules of the road .... you learn to drive.

9 You should always eat breakfast .... going to school.

10 You should always do stretches .... a run.

Students could write something like this in the speech bubbles:

Students are to **design a poster** to put by a rubbish bin. It could say something like this:

1 I'm hungry! Please feed me!

2 Please fill me up!

3 Rubbish on the ground
Brings rats around!

Students are to find the words that don't belong:

garbage
rubbish
bottles
flowers
husks
broken glass
plastic bags
peelings
bins
stink
tins
scraps
wood
ball
vegetables
paper

Me and my Responsibilities

Using our time wisely

Students should fill in the time line like this. They can shade the boxes with different colours to show overlapping hours.

6.00 a.m.					**12.00 p.m.**
Sleeping	Eating, chores	Learning	Learning	Learning	Learning
12.00 p.m.					**6.00 p.m.**
Eating, playing	Learning	Learning	Playing	Relaxing	Family
6.00 p.m.					**12.00 a.m.**
Working	Eating	Interests, TV	Sleeping	Sleeping	Sleeping
12.00 a.m.					**6.00 a.m.**
Sleeping	Sleeping	Sleeping	Sleeping	Sleeping	Sleeping

Legends

  Discuss the purpose of myths and legends.

   Read this legend to the class.

Why the possum stays up in the trees

Once, the possum lived down on the ground. One day he saw an anteater and decided to trick him.

He hid his tail under his body and said, "Look at my short tail. Short tails are best. Your long tail must be a nuisance."

The anteater looked at his tail and decided to break it off.

After he did this, the possum laughed and said, "I tricked you! Look, I have a long tail."

Then the possum ran up a tree.

The anteater was so angry that he said "Wherever you walk, I will make sorcery against you, for tricking me."

The anteater was so ashamed that he no longer had a tail that he grew spikes all over his body.

The possum became afraid of walking down on the ground, so he stayed up in the trees where he was safe from the anteater's sorcery.

This legend is from the Milne Bay area.
Ask students these questions about the legend.

1 What did the possum do to hide his tail from the anteater?

2 Why did the anteater break his tail off?

3 Why did the possum run up the tree?

4 What did the anteater say to the possum when he found out he'd been tricked?

5 Why does the possum stay high up in the trees today?

 Students are to make up their own legend about '**Why parrots are so brightly coloured**'.

 They can draw pictures of their legend.

  Read this legend to the class.

The Sleeping Island

There is an island near Karu Village, New Ireland, that wasn't always there. Many years ago, it was one hundred miles further down the coast.

It was a very different island then because it was really a man-giant. This island-giant was badly treated by the village people who used to throw all their rubbish on him.

He got up and went to the mouth of a nearby river and asked if he could rest there. The river said that it was too busy flowing and told the giant to go away.

The giant got up and moved further up the coast to another river and the same thing happened. The rivers did not want this island-giant to block their mouths.

The island-giant carried on up north until he came to two rivers that went into the sea at Karu. When he asked them if he could stay there, they said yes, and he lay down to sleep.

The strong flow of the rivers has gradually washed him out to sea and now he rests a hundred metres offshore from Karu Village. The people of this village call him Mu-Mu.

Ask students to **retell** this legend.
Find New Ireland on a map. Can students find Karu Village or the names of any of the rivers south of Karu? Can they find Mu-Mu Island?

Ask students to **write** this legend in their own words. They can draw a picture of the man-giant-island lying down in the sea.

 Dramatise this legend, using one student as the island and one as the reader.

Outdoor game: Land and Water

When the word 'land' is called, players must jump forward. When the word 'water' is called, players jump backwards. Players who jump the wrong way are out.
Then the word 'hill' can be added, and players stretch their hands above their heads.
The word 'sea' can be substituted for 'water' and players jump backwards.
When the students get good at this game, you can add words like 'bridge' (players must spread their legs wide apart).

Dog's Bones

This game is played in the Philippines.
Make a small group. Choose one player to be the 'dog'. Everyone else is a cat. The cats make a large circle around a pile of sticks, which are called 'bones'.
The dog sits beside the bones to guard them. He mustn't move from his place on the ground.
The cats try to steal all the bones without being tagged by the dog. If a cat gets touched by the dog's hands or feet, the two change places.
Begin a new game when all the bones have gone.

Me and my Responsibilities

Our country

V Black, red and yellow are traditional colours which are found in Papua New Guinean art and clothing.
The yellow bird, a bird of paradise, is culturally significant to Papua New Guineans and in full flight it represents freedom and the country's birth as an independent nation.
The five stars symbolise the Southern Cross, representing the stars Alpha, Beta, Gamma, Delta and Epsilon. Epsilon doesn't shine as brightly as the other stars because it is smaller.
The Southern Cross represents the country's geographical position in the world and its link to Australia, which also has the Southern Cross on its flag.
PNG's main rivers are the Fly River, the Kikori River, the Ramu River, the Sepik River and the Purari River.

The PNG National Anthem

O arise all you sons of this land,
Let us sing of our joy to be free,
Praising God and rejoicing to be
Papua New Guinea.
Shout our name from the
mountains to seas
Papua New Guinea;
Let us raise our voices and
proclaim Papua New Guinea.
Now give thanks to the good Lord above
For His kindness, His wisdom and love
For this land of our fathers so free,
Papua New Guinea.
Shout again for the whole world to hear
Papua New Guinea;
We're independent and we're free,
Papua New Guinea.

3 Me and my Health

Learning outcomes

Topic: Health

4.1.1 Describe changes in growth and development and plan measures to protect personal health.

4.1.3 Explain the benefits of eating from the food groups and assist in preparing healthy meals.

4.1.4 Describe the effects of harmful substances on personal health and demonstrate ways to make wise choices about their use.

Topic: Art and crafts

Make a Big Book.
Making sports medals out of clay.
'Making Things' Big Book.
Make puppets.
Make a puppet show.

Topic: Sport

Mini-Olympics.

Topic: Drama

Puppet play: Reader 9: Dr Pepe.

Topic: Cooking

Recipe day: Planning healthy menus.

Unit summary

Topics	Pictures and oral discussions	Student Book activities	Teacher Book activities	Cross-curriculum objectives	Language objectives
Healthy eating	Discuss body.	Label body. Choose correct words.	Big Book: Growing up.	Health 4.1.1 4.1.3	4.1.2 V
Vitamins	Discuss table.	Answer questions.		Health 4.1.1	
Reader 9: Dr Pepe: A Puppet Play	Read play together.		Act out play. New vocabulary. Adding 'ing'.		4.2.1 E
Eating a balanced diet	Discuss table.	Answer questions. Make up a balanced diet.		Health 4.1.3	
Healthy recipes	Read recipes.		Make recipes at a recipe day. Recipe words and measurements.	Health Cooking 4.1.3	Recipes. Text type. 4.1.4 E
Reader 10: The Magic Bilum	Read story together.		New vocabulary. Answer questions about story. Write as a play.		4.2.1 E
The digestive system	Study diagram.	Learn organ names.	The digestive process.	Health 4.1.3	4.1.2 E Making a table.
What happens if …	Read sentences.	Name preventative foods.		Health.	
Eating disorders	Discuss symptoms.	Write about fears.		Health 4.1.1	
Tastes	Discuss taste words.	Adjectives.	Taste test.	Health.	New vocabulary.
Water	Read and discuss.			Health 4.1.1	4.1.2 V

Me and my Health

Topics	Pictures and oral discussions	Student Book activities	Teacher Book activities	Cross-curriculum objectives	Language objectives
Keeping fit Letti's fitness diary	Discuss keeping fit.	Lists. Fitness diary.	Tenses.	Health 4.1.1	4.3.3 E Diary.
Having interests	Read list. Discuss.	Introduce interest.	Hobbies.	Health	4.1.2 V
Reader 11: Making Things	Read instructions.		New vocabulary. Make leis. Make windmill. Make Big Book.	Craft	Following instructions. 4.2.1 E
Celebrating successes	Read and discuss.	Write about a success.	Set goals. Mini Olympics.	Sport. Making medals. 4.1.1	Recount
Making personal goals about our health	Read and discuss.	Set personal goals. Keep a diary.		Health 4.1.1	Diary. 4.3.3 E
Worries	Discuss pictures and speech bubbles.	Give opinions.	Class discussion. Classify.	Health 4.1.1	Opinions
Grandpa is sick	Read and discuss.	Choose the correct word.		Health	
Dealing with grief	Read and discuss.	Write the five stages of grief. Write about beliefs.	Discuss personal experiences.	Health	Recount
Dealing with anger	Read through scenarios.	Write about anger.	Words relating to anger. Adverbs. Role-play conflict scenarios.	Personal development. 4.1.1	Adverbs. 4.3.2 V
Being happy	Read.	Make lists.	Words relating to happiness.	Health	4.1.2 V
Making a puppet	Read instructions.	Make puppets. Make up a play.	Act out puppet show.	Make puppet show.	4.1.2 E

Me and my Health

Topics	Pictures and oral discussions	Student Book activities	Teacher Book activities	Cross-curriculum objectives	Language objectives
Hygiene	Read and discuss.	Choose the correct words.	Practise sentences.	Health 4.1.1	
Poisons at home	Read.	Fill in missing words.	Read out facts.	Health	
Treatments	Discuss what to do if someone is poisoned.	Choose the correct word. Practise on patient.	Recovery position. Mouth-to-mouth.	Health: First aid	Following instructions.
Reader 12: Aunty Meri's New Baby	Read story together.		New vocabulary. Answer questions about story. Discuss babies and their needs.	Health	4.2.1 E
Drugs Betel nut	Discuss.	Fill in missing words.	Opinions.	Health 4.1.4	4.1.4 V
Marijuana	Discuss.	Harmful symptoms.	Opinions.		
Caffeine	Discuss.	Classifying.	Smoking. Alcohol. Draw and label body.	Health 4.1.4	4.1.4 V

Me and my Health

Me and my health

Introduce this chapter by talking about how we must keep our whole self healthy. This includes our **physical** needs, our **emotional** needs, our **social** needs, our **intellectual** needs and our **spiritual** needs.
Physical: looking after our bodies by eating healthy food, keeping fit and getting enough sleep.
Emotional: learning how to control our emotions, such as anger and anxiety, dealing with worries and grief.
Social: learning how to get on with others, caring for others, being cooperative.
Intellectual: remembering things, making good decisions, solving problems, and having interests to keep our minds busy.
Spiritual: believing in spiritual things, whether it is a belief in God or other cultural beliefs.

Healthy eating

E Students should draw Letti in their books and then label her with the correct body parts:

stomach	teeth	mouth	ears	arms	elbows	legs	chin	neck	knee
shoulders	feet	ankles	chest	wrist	fingers	nose	eyes	hair	

E Draw a body on the blackboard and ask students to label it.
Ask questions like **Where is Letti's ankle?** Choose a student to show you and write down the word **ankle** next to it.

E Make a class **Big Book** about growing up. Each student must contribute a page about themselves as they were aged two, aged seven, and now. They must draw themselves at these ages and describe the following things:

- The way they moved
- What they ate
- Their favourite games
- Their friends
- Their interests
- What they did with their family
- Their roles and responsibilities.

Me and my Health

Answers:

1 We should eat lots of **fruit** and **vegetables**.

2 We should not eat too much **sugar**.

3 We should eat lots of **rice**.

4 We should not eat too much **fat**.

5 Fish, eggs, meat and cheese **are** good for you.

Vitamins

Answers:

1 Name some leafy green vegetables. **Spinach, kumu, cauliflower, broccoli, lettuce.**

2 Which vitamin gives you energy? **Vitamin B.**

3 Which foods would you eat to make your teeth strong and healthy? **Vitamin D.**

4 What happens when your blood clots? **The blood sticks together to stop the bleeding.**

5 Which food helps us to see in the night? **Vitamin A.**

6 Which two vitamins keep our skin healthy? **Vitamin E and Vitamin A.**

7 Which vitamins do egg yolks contain? **Vitamin D.**

8 Which meat contains Vitamin K? **Pork.**

9 Which vitamins does milk contain? **Vitamins A, B, D and K.**

10 Which vitamin do nuts contain? **Vitamin E.**

11 Which vitamin does sunlight contain? **Vitamin D.**

12 Name some dairy products. **Milk, cheese, cream, butter.**

READER 9: Dr Pepe: A Puppet Play

Read through the play with the students.

New vocabulary: **hurts**, **medicine**, **beating**, **gurgling**, **junk**, **takeaways**, **greasy**, **rubbish**, **audience**, **operate**, **needle**, **thread**.

Ask students to list the 'good' and 'bad' foods mentioned in the play.

Find props in students' lunchboxes and choose people to act out the play.

Later, when the puppets are made, this play can be acted out with the puppets as a puppet show.

Teaching English

Add **ing** to these words:

hurt (hurting)	beat (beating)	gurgle (gurgling)
operate (operating)	thread (threading)	play (playing)

Eating a balanced diet

Answers:

1. Name a food that contains both carbohydrates and mineral salts. **Vegetables and fruit.**
2. Name some food that you eat at home that contains fibre. **Carrots, cabbage, cauliflower, oranges.**
3. Name some food that you eat that contains mineral salts. **Salt, fruit, vegetables, fish, meat, eggs, shellfish, nuts, seafood.**
4. Which of these foods should we eat only a little of? **Foods containing fat.**
5. We need to eat protein to make our bodies grow. What protein do you eat? How often do you eat it? **Meat, fish, beans.**
6. Think about the food pyramid you learned about in Grade 3. Which foods should we eat a lot of? **Fruit, vegetables, cereals.**

Talk about a **balanced diet** and what the students eat.
Fill in the following table on the blackboard and model the types of foods that they should be eating on most days.
For example:

	Monday	Tuesday	Wednesday	Thursday	Friday	Saturday	Sunday
Breakfast	cereal banana toast orange drink						
Lunch	bread tomato mango						
Dinner	chicken kaukau carrots kumu pineapple						
Snack	orange biscuit						

Students are to make up their own **balanced diet** using their local food (using the table format as shown above and in the Student Book). When completed, share these with the class to ensure that they are all balanced.

Me and my Health

Healthy recipes

Teaching English

Talk about these **recipe words** and their meanings with the students:

recipe	method	mix	drain	stir	grate	mash
boil	simmer	serve	ingredients	add	peel	heat
chopped	sprinkle	sliced	marinate	wok		

Discuss **measurements**:

gms (grams)	tbsp (tablespoon)	tsp (teaspoon)	mls (millilitres)
kg (kilogram)	½ (half)	¾ (three-quarters)	

E Write the following **recipes** on the blackboard.
Encourage students to bring the ingredients of the recipes to school for a **Recipe Day**. They can use these recipes or make up their own. They should choose a recipe that suits their location; for example, are you able to get fish?

Make up one of the recipes together as a class and then divide students into groups to make their own dish. When finished, everyone can have a taste.
Students can copy recipes to take home for their parents to try.

Seafood with limes

Ingredients:

1 kg white fish
4 cups mixed seafood
juice of 6 limes
¼ cup white-wine vinegar
400 mls coconut cream
2 red peppers
salt and pepper

Method:

1. Cut fish into thin strips. Mix with seafood.
2. Mix in lime juice and vinegar. Leave it to marinate for four hours. Stir it from time to time.
3. Drain off marinade.
4. Stir in coconut cream.
5. Add sliced red peppers and pepper and salt.
6. Serve with fresh salad.

(If you live in the Highlands, make up a meat recipe instead of this.)

Chinese vegetables

Any mixture of vegetables will do for this recipe.

Ingredients:

¼ cup oil
3 onions
½ cauliflower
6 sticks celery
1 green pepper
½ cabbage
2 chicken stock cubes
1 tbsp grated ginger
2 carrots
beans
1 red pepper
2 zucchini
1 cup water

Method:

1 Peel and slice all vegetables.

2 Heat oil in wok.

3 Add ginger, onions, carrots and cauliflower.

4 Add water and stock cubes.

5 Boil for 3 minutes.

6 Add beans, celery, peppers, zucchini and cabbage and cook another 3 minutes.

7 Stir.

Tropical bananas

Ingredients:

4 sweet bananas
1 tbsp brown sugar
1 tbsp butter
1 lemon

Method:

1 Melt butter in frypan.

2 Add chopped bananas.

3 Sprinkle on brown sugar.

4 Squeeze on lemon juice.

5 Stir until banana is soft.

6 Serve with ice cream.

READER 10: The Magic Bilum

Read the text with the class.

New vocabulary: **drought**, **magic**, **dream**, **spider**, **thread**, **gold**, **feast**, **evening**, **vines**, **pigeons**, **colours**, **plenty**.

Why did the people in Serrie's village have no food?

What happened in Serrie's dream?

What did the spider tell her to make her bilum with?

What things did the spider put in her bilum?

What colour was the bilum in her dream?

What did she fill her real bilum with?

Do you think it was really magic?

E Students are to write this story as a play using these characters:

Serrie Spider Mother Chief Village man

Act it out in small groups.

V Invite a student's relative to school to teach everyone how to make a bilum or a basket.

The digestive system

V Talk about the **diagram** of the digestive system in the Student Book. Students are to draw their own body and label it.

E Say the names of the organs. Students should learn them and be able to locate them on a body drawn on the blackboard.

V Talk about how the food goes through the body and how each organ has a job to do to process the food.
The organs break down the food into protein, vitamins, minerals, carbohydrates and fats. These are needed for **energy**, **growth** and **repair** to the body.
The process: The food is mixed with **saliva** and then chewed and swallowed. It goes down the **oesophagus** and into the **stomach** where it is broken down by very strong acids in the stomach.
Next the food goes into the **small intestine** where nutrients go into the bloodstream through tiny blood vessels.
The waste that the body doesn't need is stored in the **rectum** and emptied through the **anus**.
If we eat too much food or too much fatty food, it is stored in the body as fat.

 To digest our food properly, we should:

Eat our food slowly, chewing it well

Eat regular meals

Eat a balanced diet

Drink plenty of water between meals

Go to the toilet regularly to get rid of waste.

What happens if ...

Answers:
What happens if we don't eat enough Vitamin D? Name some foods we should eat to prevent rickets. **Milk, fish, egg yolks (and get plenty of sunlight).**
What happens if we don't eat enough Vitamin A? Name some foods we should eat to stop this. **Carrots, eggs, kaukau, milk, spinach.**
What happens if we don't eat enough Vitamin B? Name some foods we should eat to stop this. **Fish, seafood, chicken, meat, milk, oranges.**
What happens if we don't eat enough Vitamin C? Name some foods we should eat to stop this. **Oranges, tomatoes, cabbage, broccoli.**
What happens if we don't eat enough Vitamin K? Name some foods we should eat to stop this. **Greens, liver, pork, dairy products.**

Answers:
The child in the first picture has rickets and needs to eat **Vitamin D.**
The girl with the bleeding leg needs to have **Vitamin K** in her diet.
The boy with sore lips and swollen tongue has beriberi and needs to eat **Vitamin B**.
The child with the stick can't see very well and needs to eat **Vitamin A.**

Eating disorders

V Talk about emotional fears that we sometimes have.
Discuss **anorexia**. Does anyone know someone with anorexia?

Tastes

E If possible, bring some of the foods listed to school or ask each student to bring a different food for the **taste test**.
Cut the food into pieces. Students taste them and find the best adjective to describe them.

Bitter	Sour	Sweet	Salty	Hot/spicy	Sickly	Bland
green grapes	grapefruit	oranges	bacon	ginger	soursop	rice

Keeping fit

V Talk about activities that students could do with their families, such as playing rugby, playing basketball, swimming or running.

Letti's fitness diary

E Read through Letti's diary and discuss with students whether or not it is similar to what they do. Ask students to tell you what they do each day.
Get them to draw up a **table** like the one in the Student Book and fill it in.
You can share these diaries with the class when completed.

Teaching English

Tenses

Write these sentences on the board. Students must choose the correct tense.

1 Letti (sleep, **slept**) in and was late for school.

2 Jenifa was (**sleeping**, sleep) in Mum's bilum outside on a branch.

3 Kali was so tired after chopping the wood that he had to have a (sleeping, **sleep**).

4 Simon had a (dreaming, **dream**) about being a rock star.

5 Letti (**dreamt**, dreaming) that she was flying.

6 Mum thought she was (dream, **dreaming**) when she saw the new washing machine.

Having interests

Talk about how important it is to have interests. Take students to the library to look at books about hobbies. Ask them to choose a topic to find out about. They could do a project about a hobby that they would like to take up.

READER 11: Making Things

Read together and then choose different students to read.

New vocabulary: **leis**, **usually**, **feathers**, **dental floss**, **straw**, **measure**, **double**, **knot**, **windmill**, **square**, **triangle**, **corners**, **fold**, **spin**.

If possible, collect materials and make leis according to the directions in the book.

If you don't have enough flowers, make some out of paper.

Other materials could be used, as suggested in the book.

Go through each step together, helping students with problems.

Make windmills in the same way.

Try running with them outside to see if they spin fast in the wind.

 Students are to think of something they enjoy making.

 Make a class Big Book called **'Making Things'**.
They must **write instructions** for making something, using **steps** and **diagrams** as in *Reader 11: Making Things*. They should set out their instructions in the format shown below.
When they have finished, you could choose some students to read and demonstrate how to make their 'thing'.

 Students can then try making some of the things in the Big Book.

Write this on the board for students to copy onto paper. They must fill it in with something they want to make. It could be a kite, a bag, a spear, a hat, a pot plant container, etc.

Making a	**Diagrams**
Method: **Step 1** (text)	(picture)
Step 2 (text)	(picture)
Step 3 (text)	(picture)
Step 4 (text)	(picture)
How it works: (text)	(picture)

Celebrating successes

Talk about **achieving** and what a good thing it is to have goals in our life.
It gives us good self-esteem and gives us something to strive for.
Discuss with students things they have achieved and how they felt when they achieved them.

E Set up **goals** within the classroom for students to strive towards. You could make certificates or badges for the winning student to wear. These could be given out at a weekly school assembly or every Friday afternoon in class.
They could include:

Reading Award	Most Improved Writer	Star Speller
Maths Medal	Most Improved Player (Sport)	Good Attitude.

E Students are to write about something they made or did that made them feel good about themselves.

You could stage a **Mini Olympics** at school. Mini Olympics could consist of athletics events including:

Sprints	Long distance races	High jump
Long jump	Hurdles	Relays
Shot put	Discus	

Throwing a spear (javelin)

Archery (shooting bow and arrows at a target)

You could get some clay from the river and students could make medals for the winners.

Step 1: Shape the clay into a thin circle.

Step 2: Carve something on it with a stick or knife. You could draw the Olympic rings.

Step 3: Make a hole at the top with a nail.

Step 4: Let it dry. (This may take about a week.)

Step 5: Paint it. Medals could be painted **gold** (yellow), **silver** (white) or **bronze** (brown).

When dry, put string through the hole so the medal can be tied around a student's neck.

Making personal goals about our health

Students should fill in the table like the example given below. Read and discuss students' tables with the class.

Topic	My goals
Healthy eating	I will eat more fresh fruit and vegetables and less junk food. I will buy takeaways only once a month.
Keeping fit	I will go for a two-kilometre run every day after school. I will swim 20 lengths of the pool two days a week.
Sleep	I will turn out my light at 9.30 p.m. during the week.
Interests	I want to learn how to ride a horse. I will ask Father John at the Catholic Mission to teach me.
Drinking water	I will drink six glasses of water every day.
Worries	I won't worry about how my parents will pay for my school fees. I will try to help by making leis to sell at the market.
Dealing with anger	I will try not to lose my temper so quickly. I will try to talk quietly when I am angry instead of yelling.
Being happy	I will do more things that make me feel happy. I will play with my friends on the weekends and visit my cousins.
Hygiene	I must remember to clean my teeth every day. I must change my undies every day.

Remember to discuss this table once a week to keep students on track with their goals. You could set up a reward system for students who achieve their goals after a month.

Worries

V Have a class discussion about the types of things we worry about. Brainstorm on the blackboard for topics. These might include:

1. Family problems
2. Relationship problems
3. Worries about what will happen when you leave school
4. Financial worries – will your parents be able to keep you at school or afford to send you to a training college?
5. Health worries – is a member of your family sick?
6. Worries about whether other children like you
7. Worries about not being able to do your maths.

Students should each choose a number and then form a group with other students who have chosen the same number. They can then talk about their worry with other students who have similar worries. Talk about how these worries can be overcome. A worry shared is a worry halved.
Explain that often the things we worry about never actually happen. We can look at ways of dealing with them so that we no longer have to worry about them.

E Sometimes we can't fix the things that we worry about. In this case, we have to accept them and just get on with our lives. For example, Grandpa has cancer and he will probably die soon. There is nothing we can do to stop that, so we have to accept it.

Students are to put these words into the right columns in the table.

worry	happy	angry	excited	anxious
upset	cheerful	cross	glad	

Good feelings	Bad feelings

 Sometimes we can fix things so that we don't have to worry. For example:

Ella was worried that she wouldn't be allowed to go to the disco on Friday night. She decided to do extra chores for her parents so they would be pleased with her. She did this and they were so pleased that they let her go to the disco.

Grandpa is sick

Answers:

1 Grandpa is **sick**.

2 Mum is looking after **him**.

3 We **took** him to see the doctor yesterday.

4 The doctor said that he had a **bad** sickness called cancer.

5 Grandpa is **dying**.

6 I am **feeling** very sad. So is everyone.

7 I am **helping** Mum and Grandma to look after him.

8 Grandma is very sad too. She **cries** a lot.

9 He has **been** sick for many weeks now.

10 We **give** him medicine every day to help with the pain.

11 I **don't** like it when one of my family is sick.

12 I hope he **gets** better.

Dealing with grief

Discuss the five stages of grief. Discuss personal experiences of losing a family member or wantok.

Dealing with anger

E With the students, think up some scenarios where two people become angry with each other:

For taking something that didn't belong to them.

For not keeping a promise.

For breaking something that belongs to you.

For saying mean things about you behind your back.

Teaching English

Discuss phrases to do with **anger**: 'lost his temper', 'getting mad', 'seeing red', 'losing it', 'losing your rag', 'boiling with rage', 'seething', 'full of fury', 'in a rage'.

Introduce adverbs (words that tell how) relating to anger: angrily, crossly, furiously, bitterly.

He threw the bottle **furiously** at the wall.

Students could act this out.

Kino:	Hey Joe! You promised to come over to my house on Saturday to help me smoke the copra.
Joe:	I couldn't come!
Kino:	But you promised to help. I had to do it all by myself, and Dad was mad with me because I told him that you were going to help us.
Joe:	Well, I couldn't come.
Kino:	Well, I don't want to be your friend if you break promises!
Joe:	I don't care if you're not my friend. I've got heaps of other friends.
Kino:	No one will want you to be their friend.
Joe:	Shut up! You ugly ape!
Kino:	Don't call me names! (Slap!)
Joe:	(Slap! Punch!)

Act it out again with both friends controlling their tempers.

Kino:	Hey Joe! You promised to come over to my house on Saturday to help me smoke the copra.
Joe:	I couldn't come!
Kino:	But you promised to help. I had to do it all by myself, and Dad was mad with me because I told him that you were going to help us.
Joe:	Well, I couldn't come. I'm really sorry, Kino. I wanted to, but my Dad said that I had to help him dig up the garden for Mum. He wouldn't let me go and tell you because you live so far away.
Kino:	Don't worry, Joe. I understand!
Joe:	Tell your Dad I'm really sorry. I'll try to come over next weekend and help.
Kino:	Okay, Joe. That sounds great!

Being happy

V Have a discussion with students about what things make them happy. It is important to our health that we are happy. What can we do to make our lives happier? Write a list of suggestions on the blackboard.

Teaching English

Introduce words relating to **happiness**: cheerful, delighted, glad, joyful, overjoyed, 'walking on air', content, happy.

Making a puppet

E Ask students to follow the directions in the Student Book to make a puppet. They should paint it and dress it as instructed.

Puppet shows. Divide students into pairs and have them make up their own plays using their puppets.

Students can make a puppet show box using an old cardboard box. Make some curtains to hang in front as shown in the illustration in the Student Book.

Students should look at *Reader 9: Dr Pepe* and act out the play using their puppets in the puppet show box.

Hygiene

Students can use their puppets to practise the following sentences in English:

You must wash your hands before eating food.

You must wash your hands after using the toilet.

You must wash your hands after looking after sick people.

You must wash your hands after sneezing or coughing.

You must wash your hands after blowing your nose.

You must clean your teeth after eating.

Answers:

1. Washing your hands with **soap** is the best way to stop getting sick from germs.
2. When you cough and sneeze, cover your mouth with your **hand** or a tissue. Put the tissue straight into a rubbish bin.
3. Stay away from **sick** people so you don't catch their germs.
4. Shower or wash your **body** every day.
5. Clean your **teeth** every day.
6. Wear clean **clothes** every day.
7. Wash your **hair** every day.

Write these word activities on the board.
Choose the odd word:

sneeze	**laugh**	cough
wash	clean	**soap**
shower	**swim**	bath
teeth	**eyes**	tongue
toothbrush	**glasses**	towel

What Dr Pepe is saying:

You must clean your teeth every day, children!
And you must wash your whole body every day.
You must wash your hands before eating.
You must wash your hands after using the toilet.
You must wash your hands after gardening.
You must wash your hands after touching sick people.

More examples of **after** or **before**:

1. You must clean your teeth .... you go to bed.
2. You must comb your hair .... you get dressed.
3. You must have a shower .... you go to bed.
4. You must cut your fingernails .... they break.
5. You must dry yourself with a towel .... you shower.

Poisons at home

Answers:

You must keep medicines in a safe place because **they are dangerous to young children**.

Don't take medicine in front of small children because **they might copy you**.

Many household cleaners are **poisonous**.

Even vitamin pills can be **dangerous** if small children take too many.

Read the labels to make sure they are **safe**.

Some plants are **poisonous**.

If they are growing in your garden you must **dig** them out.

Small children can eat the berries and get **sick**.

Garden sprays can be **poisonous**.

They must be stored in the **shed/garage**.

They must be in a **safe** place.

Old bottles may still have **poison** in them.

Children might put drink in old bottles and **drink** out of them.

Treatments

E Read through the instructions of what to do if someone gets a chemical on their skin, choosing the correct words.

What to do if someone is poisoned

Answers:
Chemicals can be spilled on your **skin** and cause burns.
They can also be inhaled.
They can be **swallowed**.

Treatment of chemicals on the skin

Answers:
You should **wash** away the chemical with lots of water.
Make sure the chemical doesn't get on your **skin**.
If the person's skin is burned, they may have to see a **doctor**.
Tell the doctor what kind of **chemical** it was.

Treatment if chemical is swallowed

Answers:
Check the person is **breathing**.
Put them in the **recovery** position.
You must not make them **vomit**.
If they are not **breathing**, give them mouth-to-mouth resuscitation.
Get **medical** help.

E Choose two students to act out how to treat someone who has spilled a chemical on their arm.

V Talk about the recovery position.
Look at the illustration in the Student Book.
Demonstrate this position with a student on the floor.
Always put patients in this position if they are unconscious and you don't know what is wrong with them.

Rescue breathing (mouth-to-mouth resuscitation)

When someone is found who is not breathing, you must give them mouth-to-mouth resuscitation to get them breathing again.
Demonstrate this with a student lying on his back on the floor.

Baby (0–12 months)
Practise this on a doll.
Make sure the airway is open by pushing the head back.
Put your lips around the baby's mouth and nose.
Blow gently into the lungs, looking along the chest as you breathe.
Fill your cheeks with air and use this amount each time.
Child (1–7 years)
Make sure the airway is open by tilting the head back.
Put your lips around the child's mouth while pinching the nose.
Blow gently into the lungs, looking along the chest as you breathe. Take small breaths and don't blow too hard.
As the chest rises, stop blowing and let it fall.
Keep doing this until the child is breathing by itself.
Adult (or any person over 8 years)
Make sure the airway is open by tilting the head back.
Pinch the nose firmly closed.
Take a deep breath and put your lips around the adult's mouth.
Blow into the mouth until the chest rises.
Take your mouth away and let the chest fall.
Keep doing this until the person starts breathing. When breathing starts, place the person in the recovery position.
Students are to practise this method in pairs on the floor.

When students have practised mouth-to-mouth, ask them to write about what they did, giving instructions as above.

READER 12: Aunty Meri's New Baby

Read the text and discuss what is happening in the pictures.

New vocabulary: **expecting**, **excited**, **labour**, **drove**, **worried**, **middle**, **quick**, **breaths**, **hospital**, **scream**, **pain**.

Discuss 'going into labour' when the baby comes.

Why did Aunty Meri have to take quick breaths?

Was it painful for Aunty Meri to have the baby?

Why did Uncle Sam say it was easy?

Has he ever had a baby?

Talk with students to find out if they have any babies in their family.

Discuss the needs of babies.

Perhaps someone with a baby brother or sister could ask their mother to come to school with the baby to talk about having the baby and how she cares for it.

Drugs

Betel nut

Answers:
Chewing betel nut can lead to cancer of the **mouth**.
Chewing betel nut stains the gums and teeth **red**.
Chewing betel nut can stop you getting holes in your **teeth** but it also gives you mouth ulcers and rots your gums.
Like all drugs, it is addictive, which means you can't **stop** taking it.
It can also cause asthma, diabetes and cancer in your **organs**.

  Ask students for their opinions about whether people should chew betel nut.

  KWL about other drugs. What do students know about them?

Marijuana

  Read through the list of side effects and ask students to recall them.

Hold a discussion to find out what students think about taking this drug. Remind students of all the side effects. Has anyone they know tried it? Ask them whether they were aware of the bad effects of this drug. Would they still want to use it? What will they say if someone asks them to try it? Why?

Caffeine

Drinks in the illustration that do not contain caffeine are:

lemonade   orange juice   milk   water

 Write this on the board for the students to do.

Find the right word:

A drug that causes cancer of the mouth.

A drug that affects your mind so that you can't think properly.

A drug that gives you lung cancer.

A drug that makes your heart beat faster if you have too much.

caffeine   **cigarettes**   **marijuana**   **betel nut**

 V Talk about smoking cigarettes with the class.
KWL what they know about smoking.
How does smoking affect the body?
It can affect our respiratory system and give us lung cancer.
What about 'passive smoking'? This means that we inhale smoke if someone else smokes in our house. This can also affect us.
Have a **debate** to find out:

1 whether or not people should smoke

2 whether or not shops should be allowed to sell cigarettes.

V **Alcohol.** KWL what students know about alcohol and its effects. Does it affect anyone they know personally? How can a family be affected by someone who drinks a lot of alcohol?

E **How drugs can harm our bodies.** Draw a body and point to all the organs that can be harmed by drugs.

 Get students to draw a body and label it with captions like this:

Cigarette smoke can cause **lung** cancer.

Betel nut can cause cancer of the **mouth**.

Marijuana can affect your **brain**.

Caffeine can make your **heart** beat faster.

Caffeine can also give you **head**aches.

Alcohol can affect your **liver**.

V You can talk about **moderation**. This means that small amounts of caffeine and alcohol won't harm you, as long as you don't have too much. Other drugs like marijuana and cigarettes become addictive and you cannot stop taking them. That is when they become harmful.

4 My Responsibilities to the Environment

Learning outcomes

Topic: Environmental studies

- **4.1.1** Describe features of plants and animals that live in the environment.
- **4.1.2** Describe the impact of changes to the environment and identify solutions to potentially harmful changes.
- **4.1.3** Explain how living things interact with the environment to meet basic needs.
- **4.2.1** Describe effects of mismanaging land, sea, water and air resources and apply ways to care for them.
- **4.2.2** Investigate the consequences of waste and apply ways to minimise environmental damage.

Topic: Community living

- **4.1.4** Identify significant features of the natural environment that have an impact on people.

Topic: Art and craft

Masks.

Topic: Drama

Play: Reader 16: Trouble in the Forest.

Unit summary

Topics	Pictures and oral discussions	Student Book activities	Teacher Book activities	Cross-curriculum objectives	Language objectives
Pollution in the environment	Read and discuss.	Name things.	Go outside to find examples of pollution.	Environmental studies 4.2.1	
Air pollution	Read and discuss.	Fill in the correct word. Lists. Opinions.		Environmental studies 4.2.1	Lists.
Global warming	Read information.	Verbs. Locate countries.	Explanation.	Environmental studies 4.2.1	Reports. Speech marks. Letters. 4.3.4 V
The Carteret Islands	Read information.	Write report. Speech marks. Write letter.	Report. Speech marks. Letter. Chain reaction.	Environmental studies 4.2.1	Speech marks. Report. 4.3.1 V
Global warming changes Mosquitoes	Discuss information.	Answer questions.		Environmental studies 4.2.1	
Coral Reefs	Discuss information.	Answer questions.		Environmental studies 4.2.1	Questions. Information.
Reader 13: Coral Reefs	Read information together.		New vocabulary. Critical thinking.	Environmental studies 4.2.1, 4.2.2	4.2.1 E Critical thinking.
Drought and fire risk	Read and discuss.	Answer questions.	How to prepare for drought.	Environmental studies 4.1.4	4.1.4 V
Sea water pollution	Discuss picture.	Fill in missing words.	Collect rubbish. Write about rubbish disposal.	Environmental studies 4.2.1 4.2.2	
Fresh water pollution	Read methods of keeping fresh water safe.	Memorise steps.	Try out the methods.	Environmental studies 4.2.2	4.1.2 E
Keeping our rivers clean	Discuss pictures.	Fill in missing words.	Debate. Check river pollution. Explanations.	Environmental studies 4.2.2	Debate. 4.1.1 V

My Responsibilities to the Environment

Topics	Pictures and oral discussions	Student Book activities	Teacher Book activities	Cross-curriculum objectives	Language objectives
How we can stop pollution in our environment	Discuss pictures.	Add 'ing' to words.	Make bamboo rubbish bin.	Environmental studies 4.2.1 4.2.2	Explanations. 4.1.1 V
Where would you put this rubbish?	Discussion.	Classification.	Word search. Map. Poster.	Environmental studies 4.2.2	Classifying. Word search.
Recycling	Discuss pictures.	Fill in missing words. Write about recycling. Make junk monster.			
How the weather affects our environment	Discussion.	Fill in missing words.		Community living 4.1.4	4.1.1 V
Disasters	Discuss disasters experienced.	Research disasters.		Community living 4.1.4	Recount. Research.
Reader 14: Sebastine's Diary	Read story together.		New vocabulary. Answer questions about story.	Environmental studies 4.1.4	4.2.1 E Diary.
Precautions for natural disasters	Discuss pictures.	Choose most important items.	Discuss importance of each thing.	Community living 4.1.4	Critical thinking. 4.1.3 V
What to do in a disaster	Discuss picture.	Finish sentences.	Recount. Report. Interview.	Community living 4.1.4	Recount. Report. Interview. 4.1.4 V
Food chains	Discuss.	Fill in missing words.	Put in more arrows. Make food chains. Make animal cards.	Environmental studies 4.1.3	Critical thinking.

Topics	Pictures and oral discussions	Student Book activities	Teacher Book activities	Cross-curriculum objectives	Language objectives
Reader 15: Letti's Turtle	Read story together.		New vocabulary. Answer questions. Write report.	Environmental studies 4.1.3	4.2.1 E Report. 4.3.3 E
Food webs	Study table.	Make a food web.	Make food web using table. Classifying.	Environmental studies 4.1.3	
Looking after our environment	Discuss.	Classify: Renewable/ non-renewable.		Environmental studies 4.1.2 4.2.1	Classifying.
What we can do	Discuss.	Finish sentences. Write poem.	Explanations. Poem.	Environmental studies 4.1.2	Explanation. Poem.
Safe fishing	Discussion.	Choose correct word.	Fishing methods. Environmental rules. Posters.	Environmental studies 4.1.2 4.2.1	Making rules. 4.1.3 V
How we can protect our animals	Discussion.	Choose correct word.	Food chain. Masks. Game.	Environmental studies 4.1.1 Craft	4.1.4 V
Reader 16: Trouble in the Forest: A Play	Read play together.		Act play. New vocabulary. Answer questions about play.	Environmental studies 4.1.1 Drama	Drama. 4.2.1 E

My Responsibilities to the Environment

Pollution in the environment

 Ⓥ Discuss the importance of planting new trees when one is cut down.

Ⓥ Discuss things that cause pollution from air pollution, water pollution etc.
Ask students for examples.
Go outside the school. Can you see any examples of pollution here?

Air pollution

Answers:

1 Fumes from **cars** and trucks pollute the air.

2 Gas from **factories** pollutes the air.

3 Smoke and ash from big **fires** pollute the air.

4 **Dust** from metal roads pollutes the air.

5 All these things cause **air** pollution.

Global warming

Verbs: think, making, rise, getting, putting, making, letting, make, flooding, causing, melt, makes, rise.

Ⓔ The North Pole is also called the Arctic and the South Pole is called the Antarctic. These are made of ice and are found at the top and bottom of the world. Find them on a map of the world or a globe.

 Students can explain global warming like this:

> The pollution in the air is making the air thinner and letting in more heat from the sun. This is causing the earth's temperature to rise and this is making the ice melt at the North and South Pole.

E The rising sea level is a problem for people living on low-lying islands because the sea level is rising above the level of their land, flooding their gardens and leaving them with no food.

The Carteret Islands

  Students could write a **report** like this:

The Carteret Islands near Bougainville have a problem with rising sea levels.

Because of global warming, the sea level is rising and flooding the islands.

Joseph says, "I've got no gardens any more. I don't know how I can feed my family."

Colitha says, "The salt from the sea has killed all our crops!"

People are dying of starvation. They need help from the government.

Sometimes the land is lower than the sea and the people have to hide behind the hills of sand.

If the sea is too rough to fish, the people starve.

Five houses were washed away last year on Iesill Island when a big tidal wave came.

These people have a big problem.

Teaching English

Put in **speech marks** like this:

"I've got no gardens any more," said Joseph. "I don't know how I can feed my family."

"The salt from the sea has killed all our crops!" said Colitha.

"People are dying of starvation," said Bill. "We need help!"

"Sometimes the land is lower than the sea," said Joseph. "We hide behind the hills of sand. It's scary!"

"If it's too rough to fish," said Bill, "we starve!"

"Five houses were washed away last year on Iesill Island when a big tidal wave came," said Colitha.

E Discuss how students would write a letter to the government to ask them to help these people. It could go something like this:

To the Minister of Internal Affairs,
Port Moresby.

Dear Sir,

We have been learning about global warming at school and we have found out that the Carteret Islands north of Bougainville are being flooded because of rising water levels.

We are very worried about the people living on these islands, as their gardens are flooded and they have no crops to eat. They have to live only on fish, and if the sea is rough, they starve. They have no money and cannot escape.

Please, can the government do something to help these people?

From Grade 4 students,

……………… Primary School,
………………. Province

Students are to copy the **chain reaction** into their books like this:

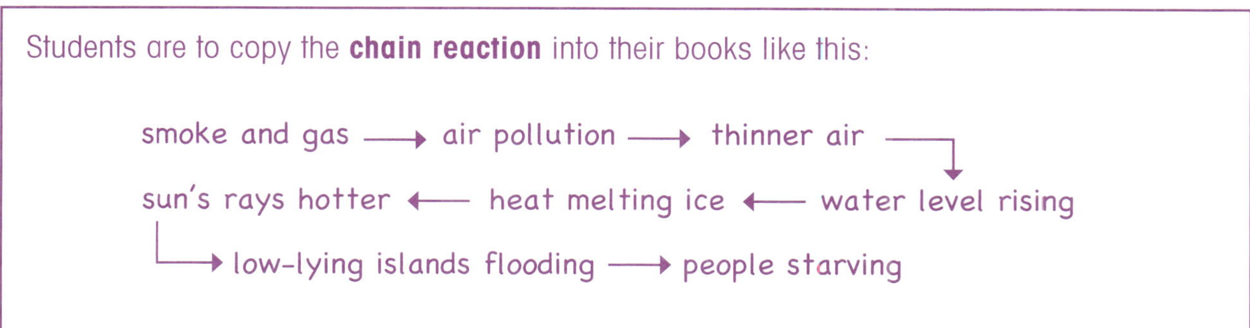

Global warming changes

Mosquitoes

Answers:
Why are mosquitoes now found in the Highlands? **Mosquitoes are now being found in the Highlands because it is getting warmer there and the mosquitoes like warm places.**
What happens if you are bitten by a mosquito? **You can get very sick with malaria or dengue fever.**
Why do plants and animals look for higher ground when it gets hotter? **Plants look for higher ground because they grow well in the heat. Animals look for higher ground because they hope it will be cooler inland.**
How will this affect us? **The plants we eat or use for medicine will move away from our environment. The animals we hunt will move away from our environment.**
Can we stop this from happening? How? **We must stop polluting the air. If everyone in the world stops, then global warming will stop.**

Coral reefs

Answers:
What does it mean when we say the reefs are bleaching? **Bleaching means that the small colourful algae that keep the coral alive are dying.**
Why is this happening? **Bleaching is happening because the water temperature is rising.**
What other things may help cause it? **Dynamiting and storm damage may also cause bleaching by destroying the algae.**
How can we stop this? **We can stop this by using safe fishing methods and keeping our air free of pollution.**

READER 13: Coral Reefs

Read through the text with the students and discuss what is happening in the pictures.

New vocabulary: **algae**, **coral**, **reefs**, **energy**, **oxygen**, **also**, **bright**, **bleaching**, **dying**, **missing**, **dynamite**, **damages**, **badly**, **anchors**.

Discuss what students can do to stop the damage to our reefs.

If you live on the coast, take the class outside at low tide to inspect the reef.

Are there any signs of pollution? Who was responsible for it?

Make up some signs to put on the beach to stop people from dumping their rubbish there.

Is the coral bleaching in your area? Look for signs.

Drought and fire risk

Answers:

What happens in a drought? **A drought means that there is no rain and everything dries up.**

Why do you think that crops and trees are more at risk from pests and disease during a drought? **Crops and trees are more at risk from pests and disease if there is a drought because they are weaker then, as they do not have enough water to keep them healthy.**

What can we do to stop forest fires from starting? **Do not light fires when there is a drought. The land burns more easily when it is dry. Strong winds can spread a forest fire.**

E Read this explanation to the students. This explains about droughts and how to prepare in case of one.

A **drought** is a long period of time when there is very dry weather. Because there is no water, animals will die, plants will not grow and wells will dry up.

Some droughts will last only a few weeks but some will last up to two years. Droughts often happen in the desert and in the hottest season. Scientists say that droughts are caused by warm tropical air falling down on the earth.

You cannot tell when a drought will happen. The only thing you can do is be ready in case there is a drought.

A reservoir of water could be built in an area where droughts are common, so that water is stored for an emergency.

People need to learn not to plant too many gardens or graze too many crops in these areas in case of drought.

Students are to answer these questions.

1 What is a drought?

2 What happens in a drought?

3 Why does it happen?

4 Where do they usually happen?

5 How long do droughts usually last?

6 What can we do to prepare for one?

Sea water pollution

Answers:

1 Oil and diesel from **boats** pollute the water.

2 Rubbish can kill **fish**.

3 Plastic can kill **fish and birds**.

4 You must not put rubbish in the **sea**.

V If your school is by the sea, walk along the beach with plastic bags and collect all the rubbish you can find. Come back to the classroom and inspect the rubbish. What is it? Where did it come from? How can we help to stop this littering from happening? If you don't live by the sea, collect all the rubbish from your local environment (outside the school). Talk about where the rubbish came from. Where should it have been put? What can we do to prevent this pollution?

E Students are to write about how they dispose of rubbish in their home. Can this method be improved?

Fresh water pollution

Ⓔ Read and **discuss** the methods of keeping our water safe.
Collect some water from a nearby river or stream.
Put some water in a pot and boil it for five minutes.
Add chlorine (if you have it) and strain the water through a cloth.
Students should taste it when it has cooled.
Students are to learn the four methods and tell their parents how to treat the river water to make it safe. In which order should these four things be done?

Keeping our rivers clean

Ⓥ Have a class discussion about pollution in our rivers. Discuss the consequences of mining and logging. You could use the internet to research this.
After researching, you could hold a **debate** about whether mining/logging is good for the country.

Ⓥ You could **organise a trip** to the nearest river with your class.
Examine the river for signs of pollution. Collect any rubbish you find.
Take a sample of the water back to school. How clean is it? Strain it through a cloth.
Walk up the river looking for signs of dead animals.

Answers:

1 **Rubbish/wood chips** from logging camps pollute the rivers.

2 Chemicals from **sprays** (pesticides) pollute the rivers.

3 Fertilisers (to make plants grow well) **pollute** the rivers.

4 Pesticides (to kill pests) pollute the **rivers**.

5 Human waste is called **sewage** (faeces).

6 It pollutes the water and makes us **sick**.

7 **Dead animals** pollute the water too.

Answers:

1 Never throw **rubbish** in the river.

2 Never go to the **toilet** in the river.

3 Never put **chemicals** in the river.

4 Take dead **animals** out of the river.

5 Never throw empty **bottles/tins/plastic bags** in the river.

6 Never throw **plastic bags/bottles/tins** in the river.

Teaching English

Explanations

An **explanation** explains why something is done.

Question: Why did you throw that bottle in the river?
Answer: I threw the bottle in the river **because I was too lazy to find a rubbish bin.**

Why did you take that dead rat out of the river?
I took the dead rat out of the river **because it was polluting the river.**

Why did you take those tins out of the river?
I took the tins out of the river **because they were polluting the river.**

Why are you taking your spear down to the river?
I'm taking my spear down to the river **because I want to spear some fish.**

Why are you and your friends going down to the river?
We are going down to the river **because we are going for a swim.**

V Students are to write an **explanation** about something they know about.
For example: How do men trap birds of paradise?

My Responsibilities to the Environment

How we can stop pollution in our environment

E Write **letters** to a local business nearby and ask them to donate rubbish bags so that you can keep the environment clean.

E **Discuss** what pollution is. What things pollute our environment? Do we have air pollution? How can we stop it? Some air pollution, like smoke from fires, cannot be helped, as fires are necessary for getting rid of rubbish.

Teaching English

Adding ing to verbs

Write this table on the blackboard/whiteboard.

Words ending in e (drop the e and add ing)	**Words ending in a consonant** (double the consonant and add ing)	**Words with two vowels** (add ing)
use	put	eat
	dig	feed

If a word ends with a blend like **ck**, **ch**, **th** or **sh**, we just add **ing**. For example:

pick – **picking**, teach – **teaching**, bath – **bathing**, rush – **rushing**

Now students should put these words in the above table:

lose	pat	clean
price	hit	peel
bite	bat	need

Answers:

1 The girl is **putting** rubbish in the bin.

2 The boy is **picking** up the rubbish.

3 The dog is **eating** the rubbish.

4 The man is **digging** a hole to bury the rubbish.

5 The child is **using** the toilet.

6 The woman is **feeding** scraps to the hens and pigs.

V Students can make a **bamboo rubbish bin** by tying bamboo pieces in a circle with bush rope or fishing line. Hang it from a tree trunk or the side of a building somewhere in the community. You could put a big plastic rubbish bag inside the container and fold the top of the plastic bag over the top to hold it in place. Make it a class chore to empty the rubbish bag and replace it regularly. (You need to make the bamboo container to fit the bag.)

Students are to write an explanation of how they made the bamboo rubbish bin. They could draw diagrams to support their text.

Where would you put this rubbish?

Fire	Garden	Hole	Pigs/hens/dogs	Rubbish dump
cardboard packaging	seaweed	broken bottle	vegetable peelings	washing machine
furniture	garden clippings	fish bones	animal bones	paint tins
rags	sheep pellets	human faeces	leftover food	old car battery
coconut husks			old bread	old bike
papers				old bath

E Write the **puzzle** on the next page on the board. Students need to find the hidden words to do with rubbish.

My Responsibilities to the Environment

n	h	l	m	n	**o**	h	o	p	t	y	d	t	p	y	r	d	f	g	u
k	k	f	g	d	**r**	z	g	f	t	h	d	**f**	**i**	**s**	**h**	f	l	t	g
j	j	t	r	e	**g**	f	**c**	**a**	**r**	**e**	f	p	s	s	p	u	m	g	e
t	**r**	a	j	s	**a**	j	p	l	e	e	d	b	a	t	**b**	i	y	u	**p**
m	**u**	f	d	v	**n**	p	l	e	e	d	**c**	**o**	**m**	**p**	**o**	**s**	**t**	w	**o**
m	**b**	v	m	h	**i**	p	g	d	h	j	o	s	w	a	**n**	i	t	r	**l**
v	**b**	o	n	u	**c**	t	y	s	q	a	i	h	n	c	**e**	t	n	s	**l**
u	**i**	g	e	d	w	**o**	**l**	**d**	**f**	**o**	**o**	**d**	g	o	**s**	r	b	e	**u**
s	**s**	r	a	r	a	s	k	j	s	i	c	t	e	r	a	a	c	a	**t**
m	**h**	e	t	y	f	o	s	a	z	**b**	**a**	**t**	**t**	**e**	**r**	**y**	f	x	**e**
k	h	**b**	**r**	**e**	**a**	**d**	s	j	e	a	l	y	t	e	r	f	o	q	n

Answers: organic, rubbish, care, pollute, bread, old food, battery, compost, bones, fish.

Students are to make a simple **map** of the local area. Take the class for a walk in the area so that students can fill in on their map what rubbish they saw and the exact location where they found it. For example:

Beach – plastic beer can holders, broken glass, empty bottles.

Students are to make posters about using rubbish bins. Put them around the local community.

Recycling

You could **recycle** the following things:

Furniture can be fixed.

Rags can be used for cleaning.

Coconut husks can be used for starting fires.

Vegetable peelings, dirt, leftover food and garden clippings can be used to make garden compost. This fertilises your garden and makes it grow well, as all the nutrients are broken down and returned to the soil to feed the plants.

Can you see other things in the picture that have been recycled?

Answers:

1. This old **tyre** is used as a swing.
2. An old **bath** is used as a flower garden.
3. Glass **bottles** are used for the edge of a path.
4. Ice cream containers are used for **paint**.
5. This jam jar is used for storing **nails**.

Students are to put a cross in the appropriate boxes. There is no right or wrong answer. Discuss the meaning before they tick the boxes.

Food scraps	☐ Put in the rubbish	☐ Make into compost	☒ Feed to pigs
Plastic packaging	☐ Put in the rubbish	☒ Reuse at home	☐ Recycle
Cardboard boxes	☐ Put in the rubbish	☒ Reuse at home	☐ Recycle
Glass bottles and jars	☐ Put in the rubbish	☒ Reuse at home	☐ Recycle
Tins and cans	☐ Put in the rubbish	☒ Recycle	
Envelopes	☐ Put in the rubbish	☐ Reuse at home	☒ Recycle
Junk mail	☐ Put in the rubbish	☒ Recycle	

Suggested answers:

You could recycle plastic packaging by using it to put food in or for storing extra bedding.

You could recycle cardboard boxes by keeping old newspapers in them. You could use the cardboard for starting fires.

You could recycle glass bottles by using them to edge a path with. You could use them to keep oil in.

You can use tins and cans to hold bait, nails or shells.

For you to do: Junk monster

Study the illustration of the Junk Monster. Students are to collect junk to bring to school. Divide students into groups of four. They must construct their own junk monster.

They can give it a name and write a story about it.

How the weather affects our environment

Floods

Answers:

1. Heavy rain makes **floods**.
2. Floods wash away the **gardens**.
3. Then, there is nothing to **eat**.
4. The river water gets **dirty**.

Droughts

Answers:

1. A **drought** is when there is no rain.
2. The **gardens** go dry.
3. The gardens **die** and there is no food to eat.
4. There is no **water** to drink.

Cyclones

Answers:

1 A **cyclone** is a bad storm.

2 The winds are very strong and the **rain** is heavy.

3 It can make a **landslide**.

4 It can damage **houses** and **gardens**.

Frosts

Answers:

1 A **frost** is very cold ice on the ground.

2 It kills plants in our **gardens**.

3 The people have no **food**.

4 We get frosts in the **Highlands** where it is cooler.

Disasters

Talk about a natural disaster that you have been in or one that you have heard about. Discuss this with the students. Research the disasters listed.

READER 14: Sebastine's Diary

Read the story with the students.

New vocabulary: **disco**, **suddenly**, **shook**, **earthquake**, **noise**, **metres**, **train**, **terrified**, **watched**, **unconscious**, **mangrove**, **hurting**, **injured**, **helicopter**.

What caused the tsunami? (An earthquake 30 kilometres offshore.)

Why did the sea disappear?

Why did Sebastine climb up the coconut tree?

Find out how many people died in this disaster.

Discuss how the lives of the surviving villagers would have been affected. (The people were afraid to go back to the water. Their gardens were ruined.)

Chain reactions

E The following account is a good example of how the environment can be disrupted by bad weather. Read and discuss with students.

> In 2004 there was bad flooding which washed away two bridges between Lae and Madang. Some of the Monia Bridge fell into the Homia River and no one could get past.
>
> Two big power pylons were knocked over and this meant that no power could get through to Madang.
>
> Old generators had to be run to give power to some of Madang, but many shops and businesses had to run their own generators.
>
> Because people had to use generators, fuel supplies ran low.

A disaster like this can cause a **chain reaction**.

heavy rain → flood → washes away bridges / power pylons collapse

→ no communications → no power → no water

→ no food → people starving → etc.

My Responsibilities to the Environment

E Read and discuss this with the students:

Manam Island, north of Madang, is an active volcano which has erupted many times.

The eruptions caused a critical shortage of food and clean water.

The volcanic ash caused huge damage to food crops, and in the worst affected areas crops were completely destroyed.

Because of the volcanic ash and contaminated drinking water, many villagers had stomach and breathing problems.

Many of the gardens on higher ground were completely buried under as much as 50 centimetres of ash.

On 24 October 2004 Manam erupted again, and 9600 people had to be evacuated to Bogia on the coast.

Some 2000 people stayed on the island, but they too had to leave when it erupted again on 8 January 2005. The lava and scoria flow swept away lots of houses and it was too dangerous for anyone to stay there.

eruption → lava/ash → gardens ruined → contaminated water → no food/water → people get sick → people evacuated to Bogia

V Discuss the **consequences** of such a disaster with the students. Students should draw on their own experiences if possible.

Students are to draw their own chain reactions to local disasters.

My Responsibilities to the Environment

Precautions for natural disasters

Emergency supplies

E Students should choose the ten most important things to put in an emergency kit. These are:

food in plastic bag

radio

torch

batteries

sleeping bags/blankets

cooking pot

chlorine bleach

soap

toothbrush

water container

 Discuss the importance of each thing.

Food: There may be no food for anyone as a cyclone may destroy the gardens, a flood could flood the gardens, etc.
Radio: You would need a radio to listen to Civil Defence who will tell you what to do in a big disaster.
Torch: You would need a torch to see in the dark if there was no electricity.
Batteries: You would need batteries for your radio and your torch.
Sleeping bags or blankets: You would need these to keep warm at night, when it is cold.
Cooking pot: You would need this to cook food and boil water.
Chlorine bleach: A very small amount of chlorine bleach added to water will kill any bacteria in the water and make it safe to drink. You should follow the instructions on the bottle.
Soap: You would need this so you could keep your body clean.
Toothbrush: You would need this so you could keep your teeth clean.
Water containers: These need to be full of fresh water in case the drinking water is muddy or unavailable.

What to do in a disaster

Answers:
Get the emergency supplies in your home. You will need these **so that you can eat, drink and keep yourself warm and safe.**
Listen to the local radio station. It will tell you **what you must do.**
Turn off all electrical machines at the main switch and close off the gas. This will stop **anyone getting electrocuted from dangerous wires.**
Fill bathtubs, sinks and plastic soda bottles with clean water. You need to do this because **you may not be able to get clean water from other sources.**

Discuss any bad storms or natural disasters that have occurred in your area over the past few years. What were the consequences to the environment? Did these conditions affect the lives of the students?

  Ask the students to write a **recount** about what they remember.

Students are to write a **report** about a local disaster.
Remind them to answer these questions:

When it happened

What happened

Where it happened

How it was dealt with.

Students are to **interview** an older person who was alive during a disaster in your area. They should ask the person questions about what happened, and then write a **report** about the disaster using the information the person told them.

Food chains

Answers:

1 The sun gives energy to the **pond weed**.

2 The pond snails eat the **pond weed**.

3 The fish eat the **pond snails**.

4 The birds eat the **fish**.

5 The crocodile eats the **fish** and the **birds**.

1 Seaweed gives energy to **limpets**.

2 Limpets are eaten by **shellfish**.

3 Shellfish are eaten by **crabs**.

4 Crabs are eaten by **seagulls**.

5 Seagulls also eat **fish**.

6 Man eats **fish** and **seaweed/shellfish/crabs**.

Students can put more arrows in the picture like this:

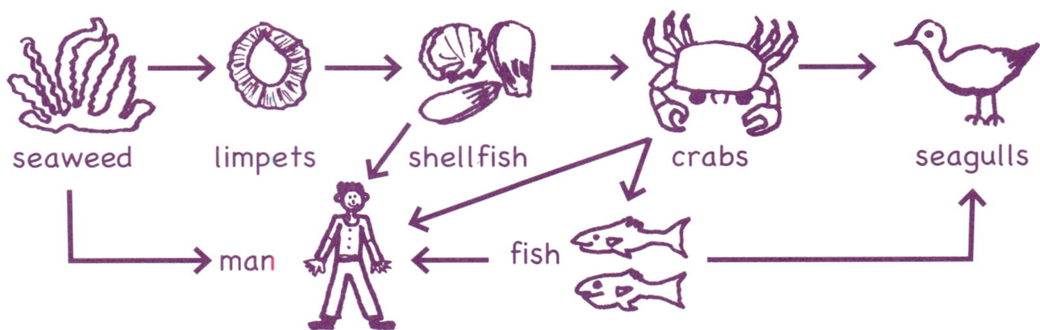

Make your own food chain:

My Responsibilities to the Environment

Ask students to write a poem about the environment.
The poem could go something like this:

Our country is so beautiful and green,
We must all try to keep it safe and clean.
We must put our rubbish into bins,
And recycle bottles, jars and tins.

Safe fishing

Answers:
In the Sepik, men fish with baskets of thorns. This is a safe way to fish.
Men on Iwa Island fish with cobwebs. This is a safe way to fish.
Some people use dynamite to kill fish. This is an unsafe way to fish.

Students are to write down why they think dynamiting is unsafe. For example, it kills everything on the reef, destroying parts of the food chain and coral and killing small fish.

Other **safe** ways of fishing include:

- Using bows and arrows to shoot the fish
- Using nets
- Using hooks and lines
- Using nets on bamboo frames
- Using plunge baskets.

Another **unsafe** way of fishing is by using the poisonous **derris roots** to catch freshwater fish, prawns and eels. The poison in the water can also kill young fish and prawns. **Gillnets** are also unsafe. They are used in lakes and rivers and kill many fish, many of which are too small to eat.

Students are to find out about **different methods** of fishing in their community. They should write about whether they think they are good or bad methods.

E Students are to think up simple **environmental rules** to make sure the birds and animals are protected in their environment.

E Make **posters** showing these rules and put them up in your local marketplace so the local people can see them.

How we can protect our animals

Answers:

1 We can protect our animals by keeping the young **alive**.

2 We can protect our animals by killing them only when we really **need** to.

3 We can protect our animals by looking after the **forest** where they live.

4 We can protect our birds of paradise by not killing too **many** for their feathers.

5 We can protect our cuscus by not killing too many for their **fur**.

6 We can protect our animals by **breeding** them.

Teaching English

New vocabulary:

Predator: the animal that hunts.

Prey: the animal that is hunted.

predator ← energy — prey

cane toad (the prey gives the predator energy) Papuan Black whip snake

READER 16: Trouble in the Forest: A Play

Read the play together.

Then choose seven students plus a reader to act in the play.

New vocabulary: **meeting**, **happening**, **either**, **everywhere**, **hours**, **gunfire**, **anywhere**, **cooler**, **coast**, **delicious**, **escape**, **enemies**, **poisonous**, **eagles**.

Ask students to find the compound words in the play: **anywhere**, **everywhere**, **Highlands**, **everyone**.

Discuss the animals in the play. Why are they leaving?

Is this what really happens when the forest is cut down?

Will they have new predators to consider?

How will this affect the food chain in the Highland regions?

Will they survive in the cooler Highlands? Discuss the effects of this, considering global warming.

Discuss the meaning of a **lucky escape**.

E Divide students into groups of 4–6. They have to make up their own **food chain** (starting with an insect or small animal), according to how many people are in their group.
Each student must choose to be one of the insects or animals. Then they must make a **mask** out of empty cardboard boxes or paper plates. Attach ears and noses with staples or tape and then paint them. Staple on a strap to hold the mask on the student's head. Cut out holes for the eyes.

E Once the masks are dry, get each group to **act** out their food chain, starting with the animal at the bottom of the food chain. He gets chased and caught by the next animal up the food chain and so on until all the animals are caught. (They could hold hands when caught.)
The students watching must write down the food chain made by that group. For example:

Group 1: worm – bird – snake – hawk.

Each group must perform their food chain while others record them.
After everyone has performed, the food chains are written on the board.
Did everyone get them right?
Now mix up the food chains. Can predators find prey from other food chains?

Notes

Notes

Notes

Notes

Notes